The Enigma of Gift and Sacrifice

PERSPECTIVES IN CONTINENTAL PHILOSOPHY
John D. Caputo, series editor

THE ENIGMA
OF GIFT
AND SACRIFICE

Co-edited by
EDITH WYSCHOGROD, JEAN-JOSEPH GOUX,
and ERIC BOYNTON

Fordham University Press
New York
2002

Perspectives in Continental Philosophy, No. 23
ISBN 1089–3938

Library of Congress Cataloging-in-Publication Data

The enigma of gift and sacrifice.
        p.   cm.
    ISBN 0-8232-2165-2 (hardcover)—ISBN 0-8232-2166-0 (pbk.)
    1. Generosity.   2. Gifts.   3. Sacrifice.
BJ1533.G4 E55   2002
177′.7—dc21   2001051111

Printed in the United States of America
02   03   04   05   06   5   4   3   2   1
First Edition

CONTENTS

ACKNOWLEDGMENTS

THE EDITORS WISH to acknowledge the support of Rice University in making possible the conference "The Enigma of Gift and Sacrifice," 26–27 March 1999, upon which this volume is based. We thank in particular Professor David Nirenberg, former director of the Center for the Study of Cultures at Rice; and former dean of the Humanities Judith Brown, whose generous financial support made it possible to bring together such a distinguished group of contributors to the conference. The project of publishing the papers presented at this conference has benefited from the ongoing encouragement of Professor Werner Kelber (the current director of the Center for the Study of Cultures at Rice University) and the Financial support of the Colgate University Research Council. We should like to thank those scholars who, during the conference, offered formal responses and commented on the conference papers now included in this volume: Professors Benjamin Lee, Diana Strassmann, Elias Bongmba, Steven G. Crowell, and Phillip Wood. We also express our appreciation to a number of graduate students—Stephen Hood, Glen Schuck, David Adcock, and specially Martin Kavka and Mary Ann Clark—whose tireless and coordinated efforts in planning and managing the numerous and necessary tasks ensured the success of the conference. Finally, thanks are due to graduate students Brett Land and Christy Flanagan for preparing the index.

The Enigma of Gift and Sacrifice

Introduction

Edith Wyschogrod

WHY THE GIFT? Why sacrifice? Why now? What meanings can be
attributed to the act of bestowing something upon another, or to
the relinquishing of something that is valued, to giving and to
giving up? The relation of gift-giving and economy, death and
sacrifice hold a special interest at the start of a new millennium,
one in which an epidermis, as it were, of images, of global economic transactions powered by new information systems, envel-
ops our world. Does this radically altered context not demand a
new discursive space for considering the issues of gift and sacrifice? If any text can be identified as generating the discussion of
gift-giving, it is Marcel Mauss's study *The Gift*, a work whose subti-
tle, *The Form and Reason for Exchange in Archaic Societies,* proclaims
its subject.[1] In explaining how people become exchangers of
goods, Mauss turns to the potlatch ceremony of the indigenous
peoples of the Northwest coast of North America and to the gift-
giving practices of some Polynesian and Melanesian peoples
(among others), practices that exhibit the obligation of "a clan,
a household, a group of people to give and to receive . . . [and
that reflect] the purely sumptuary destruction of wealth in order
to outdo a rival chief as well as his associate" (Mauss 1990, 6). By
returning to archaic society, Mauss maintains: "We shall find the
joy of public giving. . . . The system in which groups exchange
everything with one another—constitutes the most ancient system
of economy and law that we can find . . . [and] forms the base
from which the morality of exchange-through-gift has flowed"
and that, he contends, "is exactly the kind of law, in due propor-

---

[1] W. D. Halls translated the edition I used from the version published by
Presses Universitaires de France in 1950 as *Essai sur le don*. The work first appeared in 1924.

tion, towards which we would like to see our own societies move" (1990, 69–70).[2]

It could, however, be asked what can be gleaned from a work based on the ethnographies of earlier anthropologists such as Franz Boas and Bronislaw Malinowski, whose works can be read as captivating novellas but, at the same time, embody "them-us" distinctions that may today demand unsaying. Can Mauss's work become social critique, as he insists? Yet we continue to grapple with Mauss's claim that "generosity is an obligation, because Nemesis avenges the poor and the gods for the superabundance of happiness and wealth of certain people who should rid themselves of it. This is the ancient morality of the gift which has become a principle of justice" (Mauss 1990, 18). Analytic philosophers may detect similarities to John Rawls's statement that "inequalities of wealth and authority are just only if they result in compensating benefits for everyone and in particular for the least advantaged members of society" (Rawls 1971, 14–15). Mauss also claims of the groups he considers: "To refuse to give or receive is tantamount to declaring war, rejecting a bond of alliance and commonality" (Mauss 1990, 13).

Further elaborating upon the theme of excess, Georges Bataille, whose views have influenced much contemporary discussion of gift and sacrifice, interprets the expenditure of surplus in terms of the acquisition of power in which the subject commodifies, as it were, her or his virtue, "enriching himself with a contempt for riches. . . . what he proves to be miserly of is in fact his generosity" (Bataille 1991, 69). In communities in which production is the principal goal, Bataille discovers a hidden aporia: the otherness of death. Such communities claim that they serve the principle of utility when, in actuality, they have run wild and create only death through war and extermination. René Girard, whose own views on sacrifice have elicited considerable comment,

---

[2] The unusual interest in the question of the gift has generated a number of recent works devoted wholly or in part to the issue. Of special interest are *The Gift: An Interdisciplinary Perspective* (Aafke 2000), a collection of essays that tracks the notion of gift from Mauss to recent social scientific accounts; and *God, the Gift and Postmodernism* (Caputo and Scanlon 1999), a collection that includes a conversation between Derrida and Marion about the theological implications of giving.

says of Bataille that his "apparent decadent aestheticism . . . the only spice still capable of stimulating the jaded appetite of modern[s]," is transcended insofar as violence is eliminated through sacrifice.

But what are we to make of giving and sacrificing, acts that we shall see can be construed in multiple ways, in a postmodernity that has been described by Baudrillard and others as arriving after the end of time as we have known it? Are we caught between "simulation," the unity of closed systems that can only be mimed, and "negentropy," the event we are now experiencing that follows upon increased complexity, the arising of the need for noise and distraction in the human "living machine," as Dietmar Kamper puts it? Is the gift to be construed as part of the circuitry of a closed system of exchange, or can it be seen as negentropic, disturbing the structure of political, economic, and social closure, as a refusal to think within the ossification of a closed system (Kamper 1989, 98–100)?

It is the aim of the present volume to bring multi-disciplinary perspectives to bear upon the themes that are its subject, to interrogate their enigmatic mode of disclosure that say and unsay the claims of rational social, political, and economic discourse and behavior. At a conference, "The Enigma of Gift and Sacrifice," held at Rice University, 26–27 March 1999, a group of distinguished scholars met to interrogate these claims from the vantage points of philosophy, anthropology, literary studies, and feminist discourse. The earlier versions of the essays in this collection that were presented there generated intense discussion. The introductory remarks that follow are not intended to function heuristically, to constitute an enframing or unifying discourse with regard to these essays—they speak eloquently for themselves—but rather to ponder the contemporary conceptual context in which they have arisen.

I

For Jean Baudrillard, we live in a state of hypertrophied growth, one of excess not in Bataille's sense of lavish production, but rather as one in which materiality is reduced, miniaturized, and time-compressed into nanoseconds. Time is "the real bomb" that "immobilizes things in eerie retrogression," Baudrillard proclaims (1989, 35). Arguing that the "hyperreality of the code and of simulation" absorbs what had heretofore been perceived as real, he insists that one cannot turn to the subversive theoretical structures that guided modernity, but rather to the randomness of simulacra, floating images without originals, to symbolic disorder, to death itself. Baudrillard does not back down on these claims, yet, against this backdrop of devastation and as intrinsic to it, he posits the liberating potential of the gift, not as instantiating but, astonishingly, as annihilating what he calls an enslavement to value. Thus Baudrillard:

> Beyond the topographical and economic schema of psychoanalysis and politics, which always revolve around . . . production (whether material or desiring) on the scene of value, we can still perceive the outline of a social relation based on the extermination of value. For us . . . its radical utopian version is beginning to explode . . . in the vertigo of a revolt which has nothing to do with revolution or the laws of history or . . . the "liberation" of a "desire" (1988, 119).

It is in this light that Baudrillard interprets the hypotheses of Fernand de Saussure and Marcel Mauss. More subversive than Freud and Marx, Saussure's analyses of the sign and Mauss's account of the gift bring to the fore "not just curiosities of linguistics and anthropology . . . but the outline of a single form . . . that relates political economy and libidinal economy . . . a beyond of value, of the law of repression and of the unconscious" (Baudrillard 1988, 119). Does this mean that the utility of any theorizing about the gift and sacrifice is mooted, to be renounced in favor of the "pure event," one without "precedent and without consequences" (192–93)? Perhaps. Yet surprisingly, Baudrillard does not shrink from the historical chore of chronologically tracking the order of simulation from the classical and industrial eras to the present.

To be sure, Baudrillard rejects economic, psychological, and structuralist readings of Mauss's work, maintaining that we must radicalize the theory of the gift against itself, think "the reversibility of the gift in the countergift, of exchange in the sacrifice of time in the cycle, of production in destruction, of life in death . . . in all domains reversibility." For Baudrillard this reversal takes on the form of the symbolic, of "extermination and death" (1988, 119–20).

It would seem that the individual self is either evacuated or emptied in the ecstasy of death. Still, one could say: *sic et non.* To be sure, we are waste products in consonance with the transformation of the natural world into residues, waste (Baudrillard 1994, 78–91). Nevertheless it must be noted that, in his account of the consumer society, Baudrillard invokes the idea of the individual that he undermines elsewhere. Contending that although technology has replaced the individual as producer, individuality is needed in the context of consumption. "Competition" has given way to globalizing tendencies, a process in which the person becomes *ego consumans.* "Consumption is a powerful element in social control (by atomizing individual consumers); yet at the same time it requires the intensification of bureaucratic control over the processes of consumption" (Baudrillard 1988, 52–53). An inherited tradition of altruism, of gift-giving, Baudrillard contends, is invoked by the consumer society to mask and soften the impact of consumption: the gift as handout.

In this respect, there is considerable proximity between Baudrillard's view of consumption and that of Bataille, who contends that the rules of rank that governed the gift-giving of the potlatch have now been transcended: "The present forms of wealth make a shambles and a human mockery of those who think they own it. In this respect present-day society is a huge counterfeit, where this truth of wealth has slipped into extreme poverty, a lie that destines life's exuberance to revolt" (Bataille 1991, 76–77). The meaning of wealth can only be discovered in "the somber indifference of the individual" (76–77).

Is Bataille's view not also premonitory of one of Baudrillard's most distinctive ideas, that of the fatal strategy? In a claim that seems paradoxical, the cunning of the object is always victorious over the subject. Fate and not design is at the heart of every strategy, a fate that is without telos yet dynamic and that frustrates the objectives of the subject. Morality itself is caught up in this fatality: it "is no longer moral stasis but moral ecstasy" (Baudrillard 1988,

205). Is fatality in Baudrillard's sense not a version of Bataille's idea of the revolt that is destined?

The notion of the countergift that we have seen as intrinsic to Baudrillard's account of gift and economy is not absent from the work of Derrida. In his discussion of the politics of friendship, Derrida alludes to the Sage who in playfulness turns himself into a fool, an inversion that Derrida sees as a giving of self. The Sage "makes himself into a gift, feigns, lies, disguises himself, masks himself out of friendship for mankind" (Derrida 1997, 60). But it can be argued that this gift-giving too must be reversed. Consider a recent icon of popular TV drama, *Survivor,* in which a state of nature is simulated in order to determine who will, through wit and will, outlast all the others, and this under the glare of invisible TV cameras. To win, friendship for the other must sometimes feign hostility toward the other in the interest of that other (a trick Kierkegaard had already noticed in the mother's blackening of her breast to wean the child). On the other hand, hostility may actually be hostility itself that can, in this climate of ruse and trickery, be misinterpreted as merely simulated hostility. Derrida notes that the Sage presents himself as an enemy "to hide his enmity . . . feigning to be precisely what he is" (60). Are these inversions not conveyed in the homonymy of the English "gift" and the German *Gift,* "poison"?

What, one may ask, are the implications for the understanding of gift-giving if, as has been argued by Jean-Luc Nancy and others, we cannot meaningfully speak of the individual subject as it had been understood in a tradition extending from Descartes to Hegel? Are we not compelled to ask "Who comes after the subject?" Is the subject an empty grammatical placeholder? If, in the light of a deconstructed self, "interiority, self presence, consciousness of mastery, of the individual or collective property of an essence," as Nancy alleges, who gives and who receives (Nancy 1991, 4)? Nonpersonal modes of individuation that no longer constitute persons or egos, which Gilles Deleuze designates as ecceities or haecceities, have replaced the subject.

Along similar lines, analytic philosopher Derek Parfit argues that, although we ascribe that which is thought to thinkers, we cannot conclude from the content of our experience that a thinker is a separately existing entity. What we call a person refers to a psychological connectedness and continuity that may be ascribed to any number of causes, such as brain states (Parfit 1984, 215).

Is this not what Baudrillard means by the "simulation of an infinite trajectory" (1994, 2)? Have we then entered a discursive space aptly described in the Indian text of the Bhagavad Gita, a space in which the illusoriness of a substantive self is undone when the god Krishna urges a reluctant Arjuna to engage in battle by invoking the apothegm: "There is no slayer and there is no slain." Could it not be argued that there is in each of these accounts of the demise of the subject a sacrifice, an ardent pursuit of death? Has Bataille not in some sense described this self-emptying in his interpretation of the sacrifice of "the man-god" who dies and is redeemed, but in dying eludes the being of the sovereign self, of the me that is extinguished. For Bataille, "the horror of the cadaver and . . . of blood tie the *me* that dies more obscurely to an empty infinity" that is itself projected as death and dissolution (Bataille 1985, 133). It is, he declares, as sumptuary sacrifice that death of the me is to be lived "with the avidity of sadistic ecstasy" (134).

It is, of course, no arbitrary link that ties the gift to sacrifice and death, as Derrida notices. In analyzing the work of Czech philosopher Jan Patocka, Derrida considers "whether his discourse on the gift and on the gift of death is or is not a discourse on sacrifice and on *dying for the other*" (Derrida 1995, 33).[3] Derrida needs no reminder of the way in which this enigma is played out in connection with Abraham's sacrifice of Isaac. In Kierkegaard's famous gloss of Gen. 22:1–19, Abraham is seen to have a duty to obey the moral law that is binding upon all, a law that would interpret human sacrifice as murder. However, if this law is countermanded by God, the moral law itself becomes a temptation. Kierkegaard's knight of faith, Abraham, does not demur in the interest of ethics but says yes to God's command.

In the same essay, "The Gift of Death," Derrida writes that sacrifice is, as in Mauss, linked with economy. Abraham's decision is seen as a gamble:

---

[3] In his preface, translator David Wills notes that Patocka was affiliated with the Charta 77 Human Rights Declaration of 1977 and died of a brain hemorrhage after extended police interrogation.

> In renouncing . . . the life of his son [as precious as his own],
> Abraham gains or wins. He risks winning having renounced win-
> ning . . . expecting nothing that can be given back to him. . . .
> [Yet] it is given back to him because he renounced calculation.
> Demystifiers of this superior or sovereign calculation that consists
> in no more calculating might say that he played his cards well (Der-
> rida 1995, 96–97).

Is loss without recompense not tied to the win-or-lose law of the circulation of goods in an economy? "Through the law of the father economy reappropriates the *an*economy of the gift, or what amounts to the same thing, a gift of death" (Derrida 1995, 97). For Emmanuel Levinas, who opens the way to a reading of the gift as radical sacrifice of the self, Abraham's sacrifice is to be read otherwise. From the standpoint of the world, the inner drama of Abraham is indeed a scandal. It is a drama in which truth is self-enclosed, a truth of inner consciousness that fails to open the human being to the other. There can thus be no self-giving, no "putting in question of the I by the Other" that, for Levinas, signifies the ethical relation to the other as one of total self-donation (Levinas 1996, 73). In the worry about sacrificing not the self but another, traces of Moses Maimonides's wariness of sacrificial cults can be discerned as wending their way errantly through Levinas's account. Because sacrificial cults are seen as intrinsic to the polytheism of the ancient world by Maimonides, sacrifice is, for him, suspect. Appealing to Samuel, Isaiah, and Jeremiah, Maimonides concludes, "The prophets distinctly declared that the object of the sacrifices is not very essential, and that God does not require them" (1904, 325). Thus Maimonides proclaims that the object of the trial of Abraham is to convey a pedagogy, to teach humans what they should do or believe, but that the act of sacrifice itself is not the end desired. Without touching on the rationalistic thrust of Maimonides's interpretation, Levinas adopts a certain suspicion of the sacrifice of Abraham, contending, "Perhaps Abraham's ear for hearing the voice that brought him back to the ethical order was the highest moment in the drama" (Levinas 1996, 74). But far from abjuring sacrifice, Levinas reverses the order of sacrifice—a reversal Maimonides would not condone—contending that it is the self that must be willing to surrender in the interest of the other.

Yet if Levinas rejects Kierkegaard's account of Abraham's sacrifice, he does not hesitate to credit Kierkegaard with challenging the received view that belief is imperfect knowledge, whereas genuine knowledge yields truth, truth that cannot be contested. For Kierkegaard, Levinas maintains, knowledge itself is always already fissured, rent by recurrent inner doubt. Thus Levinas credits Kierkegaard with bringing to the fore what Levinas calls persecuted truth in contrast to truth triumphant, the former opening the way for sacrifice not *of* the other, but of the self *for* the other. Such sacrifice is not in the interest of ecstasy, as it is for Bataille, nor is it sacrifice in response to a heavenly voice. Rather, it is sacrifice in the prosaic interest of responsibility: "I have not done anything and I have always been under accusation—persecuted. . . . The word *I* means *here I am*, answering for everything and everyone" (Levinas 1981, 114).

For Levinas, one cannot evade the other's sheer existence, an existence that acts upon the self as a command to divest the self of itself and to willingly substitute for the other. Yet, it must be asked, to become a giver, must there not be a reversal of the order of the gift? Must I not receive a prior gift bestowed upon me by the other, the gift of her or his sheer alterity through which I become a giver? And insofar as the other must be altogether other and, as such, cannot become an object of knowledge to the self, must we then not say there is no giver and there is no gift? For Levinas, "the way that the Other has of seeking my recognition while preserving his incognito, disdaining recourse to the wink-of-an-eye of understanding or complicity, this way of manifesting himself without manifesting himself, we call enigma" (Levinas 1996, 70).

II

The first section of this work, "The Economy of Sacrifice," considers the social, economic, and political function of that which lacks utility in the context of an emergent global economy. Can value be attributed to what remains outside the sphere of exchange? If so, must not such objects, if they are to influence the sphere of economy, be both outside and inside that economy? In pursuing these questions, objects seemingly as disparate as the sacred artifacts of Melanesian societies and contemporary art-works are considered by various contributors in their relation to exchange and to sumptuary expenditure.

In chapter 1, Maurice Godelier finds in Mauss's work a clue to determining whether there are conditions intrinsic to the life of societies that transcend the interests of the market. A neglected aspect of Mauss's theory, that of non-agonistic giving, is con-trasted with the agonistic practices of the potlatch that are driven by competition in the interest of maintaining wealth and social hierarchy. Godelier explores the non-agonistic relation of giver and recipient in which gifts feed obligations that, in turn, set up a flow of services and "reciprocal obligations of solidarity." Sacred objects, he notes, are neither sold nor given, but are needed for "the production and reproduction" of societies. Godelier's ac-count can be read as the post hoc constitution of an origin, that of social existence. To be sure, this origin is now camouflaged by the laws of exchange, for the significations of sacred objects may be coopted by the forces they have produced. Yet Godelier con-cludes that the market has its limits. In selling, a person is alien-ated from what is sold; in giving, something of the person remains in the object (as was believed by some Melanesian peoples); and in retaining the sacred object, thing and person together consti-tute a historical identity that is socially transmitted.

George Marcus's essay, chapter 2, might be read as a response to Paul Virilio's question "How can I get nowhere or at least as close to it as possible . . . but with increasing speed?" (Virilio 1989, 114). Pointing to the futility of metaphors of autochthony in a world in which the hypertrophied speed of circulation de-mands interpretation, he looks beyond the obvious heirs of Mauss to develop an account of circulation as a form of culture. The "market fundamentalism" of George Gilder as well as that of George Soros, who does not gainsay the maximization of profit while engaging in philanthropic enterprises, transcend tradi-tional accounts of exchange and demand radical reexamination. Bourdieu's analysis of change as a concealed/concealing manage-ment of time, as well as Bataille's critique of utility and rationality, are seen by Marcus as helpful in that they explore the incompatibility of the discourse of social commitment and the dominance of circulation.

In a candid and original critique of the logic of the gift in chapter 3, Mark C. Taylor suggests that academic discourse about the gift attributes to itself a high-mindedness grounded in an inutility that purports to elude the economy of exchange. Turning first to Derrida's critique of Bataille, Taylor exposes the logic of giving as a play of inversions in which Hegelian dialectic is overturned to become the logic of capitalist economy, the negation of a negation that "turns every loss into a gain." The distinction between the useful and the useless is seen to segue into the contrast between purposiveness and the purposeless that, in turn, leads to the ascription of purposiveness without purpose to the artwork in Kant's third *Critique.* At a time when the all-embracing mechanisms of the marketplace supplant an earlier patronage system, value is attributed to the uselessness of the artwork. Similarly, Taylor maintains, the academic profession's regard for inutility and its critique of calculation are the ploy created by an elite that purports (often self-deceptively) to elude market forces while profiting from the commodification of knowledge.

The second section of this collection, "Community, Gift, and Sacrifice," considers the ways in which communities are shaped by language and gender. Whether conceived as radically altruistic or the result of socially constituted roles, giving is imbricated in social existence. As Foucault would have it, the relation of language and power, how one statement appears rather than another at a given time such that constellations of power and agency are manifested through it, requires explanation. Admittedly, this is an explanation imbricated in its own rules. Language is a system not only of signs, but of practices contingent upon rules that determine the possibilities of utterances and actions.

A linguistic account of gift-giving in an Indian village by Stephen Tyler, chapter 4, considers the gift in the context of the grammatical configuring of propositions. Tyler maintains that agency enters into the structure of words to determine the positions of giver and recipient. Propositional structure also articulates psychological conditions, motivation, expectation, and the like. But far from arguing for grammatical determinism, Tyler considers the relation of language to social context. As a case in point, he shows how the ideas expressed in the *dharmasastras* (treatises on the ordering of social existence) are actually lived in the *jajmani* (sacrificial) system of some Indian villages. He points not only to reciprocal giving but also to the role of sacrifice as a way of getting rid not of surplus, but of inauspiciousness. Tyler does not deny the processes of depersonalization in contemporary existence, but opens the possibility of parallel realities in which intentions still inhere.

In chapter 5, an analysis of the relation of language and giving, Genevieve Vaughan "looks at the world through women's eyes." Mothering, stigmatized as mindless by the discourses of patriarchy, is reconnected to social existence by viewing childcare as unilateral gift-giving. Vaughan contrasts exchange value—often interpreted as the basis for equality and justice in social transactions—with gift-giving. In fact, exchange requires scarcity to subsist, while gift-giving requires abundance. Pointing to the scripting of male and female roles as nonbiological, she shows that women who adopt male roles in the world of work are rewarded. Turning to language as a mediating link between the world of "mothering, symbolic gift exchange, and commodity exchange," she maintains that words are gifts, or, put otherwise, gift-giving can be seen as the very logic of language. In an analysis of the ways in which the abstraction of money establishes equivalences and is made to define persons, Vaughan hopes that a new social order based upon unilateral gift-giving can unsay the rules of patriarchy.

In the final section of this collection, "The Gift of Philosophical Discourse," the ambiguities inherent in giving are explored. When seen otherwise than as an extrapolation from the resources of philosophy and theology, the gift can be interpreted as unsaying the rationality of received traditions, a provocation that is a pharmakon in Derrida's sense of gift and poison. Gift-giving can also be seen as inseparable from the relation to alterity: there is gift through the existence of the other, a recipient, and, conversely, there is another who is understood as the one to whom something is given. If so, does not the gift relation presuppose the very alterity it establishes? Can one give the self if one does not already have it? Perhaps the gift is impossible. Can these aporias be thought otherwise?

In chapter 6, thinking of and through the gift, John D. Caputo explores a radically new way for understanding the ecstases of time, the symmetries and asymmetries of past and future, and the thorny question of the relation of grace to justice. Extending Derrida's account of the gift, Caputo's rich and complex analysis brings to light the relays involved in the relation of giving and forgiving such that the paradoxes of the gift, that which renders the gift both possible and impossible, are seen to be replicated in the aporias of forgiveness. Caputo considers the issue of whether, in the religious traditions of Judaism and Christianity, the conditions for forgiveness are regulated. If so, do we not, instead of forgiving sinners, forgive those who, in meeting these conditions, become non-sinners? If forgiveness is not to be swallowed up in relations of exchange, it must be unconditional. Caputo finds resources for grasping the aporias of forgiveness in the Lukan parable of the tax collector and the Pharisee and in the medieval philosopher Peter Damian's account of divine omnipotence. Because, for Damian, God can reverse the order of time, from God's eternal point of view, the sinful deed is rendered moot, thereby reducing something that exists, the offense, to something that is not. Turning from the standpoint of the offended to the offender, Caputo maintains that the latter must accept unconditional responsibility not as irreversible, but as opening on to a new creation that is always yet to come, a forgiveness as "a giving of time."

Jean-Joseph Goux argues that, in neglecting Seneca's treatise on the gift or "the kind deed," Derridean analysis may have overlooked some aspects of giving that inhere in the relation of the gift to alterity. Goux recognizes that the semiotic that renders Seneca's account understandable is subverted by Derrida's deconstruction of the sign, and thus of the gift as the signified. Yet in denying the possibility of giving a gift to oneself, Seneca may escape this charge by isolating the moral moment of the gift not in the signified, but rather in an intrinsic relation to the alterity of the other. A tripartite analysis of the gift in terms of profit, munificence, and intention leads Goux to contrast the pure gift, giving for the advantage of the recipient who cannot return it, with usury as reclamation of a debt with interest, as well as with ostentatious giving. It is not, for Seneca, the gift as object, but what transpires in the souls of giver and recipient that is significant. The

return of pure gifts is not effected materially, but rather as a gratitude that establishes not commensurability but a relationship with
the giver.

In chapter 7, the questions of whether the gift is, in fact, impossible and of whether the self can become a gift are interpreted
in Adriaan Peperzak's thought-provoking essay, "Giving." Noting
that the gift has become a source of amazement to philosophers,
Peperzak welcomes this development but remains apprehensive
about recent hyperbolic characterizations of the gift. In the discourse of exaggeration, the gift is caught between "cynicism and
a fideistic leap to the impossible." Turning to the sources of his
own amazement, Peperzak analyzes authentic generosity, decep-
tive or hypocritical giving, and the "normalcy of mixed giving."
In an effort to depart from the unrealizable ideal of the pure gift,
he argues that the dissymmetry of self and other that mandates
respect for the other does not preclude the "self's deserving a
similar respect." In a move that may remind the reader of Kant's
claim that joy can supervene upon but not motivate moral acts,
Peperzak rejects the argument "that posits a contradiction between giving and the enjoyable response it elicits."

The differing perspectives reflected in these essays suggest that
discourses about the gift cannot be rendered commensurable.
Nor can the issue of gift-giving be brought to closure through the
positing of agreement about "first principles" on the spurious
premise that without such principles, gift and sacrifice could not
be thought at all. The innovative contributions in this collection
cannot be said to inaugurate a new discourse, in that beginnings
are always already in question as breaching an existing order.
Must we not continue to ask what, then, in giving gives itself to be
questioned? Can we think pure givenness? Or are we, in remem-
brance of Heidegger's admonition, to ponder the indissolubility
of thinking and thanking (*Denken und Danken*), to give thanks for
that which "gives us to think"?

BIBLIOGRAPHY

Aafke, Komter, ed. 2000. *The Gift: An Interdisciplinary Perspective.*
Amsterdam: Amsterdam University Press.

Bataille, Georges. 1991. *The Accursed Share: An Essay on General Economy*. Vol. 1, *Consumption*. Trans. Robert Hurley. New York: Zone Books.

———. 1985. *Visions of Excess: Selected Writings, 1927–1939*. Trans. Alan Stoekl. Minneapolis: University of Minnesota Press.

Baudrillard, Jean. 1994. *Illusion of the End*. Trans. Chris Turner. Stanford: Stanford University Press.

———. 1989. "The Anorexic Ruins," in Dietmar Kamper, ed., *Looking Back on the End of the World*. New York: Semiotext(e), Columbia University Press.

———. 1988. "Consumer Society," in Mark Poster, ed., *Selected Writings*. Trans. Charles Levin. Stanford: Stanford University Press.

———. 1988. "Fatal Strategies," in Mark Poster, ed., *Selected Writings*. Trans. Charles Levin. Stanford: Stanford University Press.

———. 1988. "Symbolic Exchange and Death," in Mark Poster ed., *Selected Writings*. Trans. Charles Levin. Stanford: Stanford University Press.

Caputo, John D., and Michael Scanlon, eds. 1999. *God, the Gift, and Postmodernism*. Bloomington: Indiana University Press.

Derrida, Jacques. 1997. *Politics of Friendship*. Trans. George Collins. London: Verso.

———. 1995. *The Gift of Death*. Trans. David Wills. Chicago: University of Chicago Press.

Girard, René. 1972. *Violence and the Sacred*. Trans. Patrick Gregory. Baltimore: Johns Hopkins University Press.

Kamper, Dietmar. 1989. "Between Simulation and Negentropy," in Dietmar Kamper, ed., *Looking Back on the End of the World*. New York: Semiotext(e), Columbia University Press.

Levinas, Emmanuel. 1996. "Enigma and Phenomenon," in *Basic Philosophical Writings*. Trans. Alphonso Lingis as revised by the editors, Adriaan T. Peperzak, Simon Critchley, and Robert Bernasconi. Bloomington: Indiana University Press.

———. 1996. *Proper Names*. Trans. Michael B. Smith. Stanford: Stanford University Press.

———. 1981. *Otherwise Than Being or Beyond Essence*. Trans. Alphonos Lingis. The Hague: Martinus Nijhoff.

Maimonides, Moses. 1904. *Guide for the Perplexed*. Trans. M. Friedlander. New York: Dover reprint, 2000.

Mauss, Marcel. 1990. *The Gift: The Form and Reason for Exchange in Archaic Societies*. Trans. W. D. Halls. New York: Norton.

Nancy, Jean-Luc. 1991. Introduction, in Eduardo Cadava, Peter Connor, and Jean-Luc Nancy eds., *Who Comes after the Subject*. New York: Routledge.

Parfit, Derek. 1984. *Reasons and Persons*. New York: Oxford University Press.

Rawls, John. 1971. *A Theory of Justice*. Cambridge: Harvard University Press.

Virilio, Paul. 1989. "The Last Vehicle," in Dietmar Kamper, ed., *Looking Back on the End of the World*. New York: Semiotext(e), Columbia University Press.

1

The Economy of Sacrifice

1

Some Things You Give, Some Things You Sell, but Some Things You Must Keep for Yourselves: What Mauss Did Not Say about Sacred Objects

Maurice Godelier

MY PROBLEM, in this essay, is to understand why there are some things one sells, others one gives, and yet others that can be neither sold nor given, but that must be kept and transmitted. It is clear that the reasons do not reside in the things themselves. The same object may successively be bought as a commodity, circulated in gift exchange, and ultimately hoarded in a clan treasure as a sacred object and, as such, withheld for a time from any form of circulation, market or nonmarket. Michel Panoff showed this nicely in his study of the seashells used by the Maenge of southern New Britain.

In choosing to explore this theme, I am evidently situating myself within the current of anthropological history, and my point of reference can be only one of the great moments in this history, Marcel Mauss's indispensable text published in 1924, his *Essai sur le don*. In a moment I will trace the context in which the *Essai* was written, but first I would like to outline the reasons that moved me to return to the analysis of these problems.[1] These reasons are three in number. First of all what I discovered in the Baruya soci-

---

[1] This essay follows the analyses and conclusions developed in my book-length study of these problems, *The Enigma of the Gift*, trans. Nora Scott (Chicago: University of Chicago Press, 1999).

ety, then my twenty-year-long dialogue with Annette Weiner and
my reading in 1992 of her *Inalienable Possessions: The Paradox of
Keeping While Giving,* and finally the context of the globalization
of the Western capitalist system. I will say a few words about each
of these contexts.

The Baruya provided me with the example of a society that still
practiced gift exchange—the exchange of women, for example—
but that did not have potlatch. They produced also a sort of "cur-
rency-commodity," salt, which they bartered with neighboring
tribes for tools, weapons, feathers, and other goods that they did
not produce themselves. But salt was never used as money within
Baruya society; there it circulated in the form of gifts. Lastly there
were sacred objects, which the Baruya treated with the utmost
respect, the *kwaimatnie,* used in the boys' initiation ceremonies
and presented as gifts from the gods to their ancestors, gifts they
might not give to other human beings.

Now, Annette Weiner. Our friendship dates back some twenty
years, as I have said, to the publication in 1976 of her *Women of
Value, Men of Renown,* which transformed the view we had inherited from Malinowsky of the way society worked on Kiriwina. It
was not only an anthropological interpretation of the *kula* that
was renovated by her discovery of two notions with which Malinowsky was unfamiliar, *kitoum* and *keda.* It was also, and especially,
the fundamental role of women in this society, as she revealed it
in her analysis of the notion of *dala,* the substance handed down
by the founding female ancestors of the clan, an everlasting substance circulating through the women and that constituted the
timeless identity of the clans. This was a dazzling demonstration
that a feminist perspective on anthropology brings out the si-
lences, the gaps, the distortions implied by all-too-often exclusively male observations that are unaware of the consequences
this bias entails. But we owe her more than simply a new interpretation of one particular society. With the publication in 1992 of
her last book, *Inalienable Possessions,* Annette Weiner initiated a
reexamination of the whole problem of the interpretation of gift-
giving. She was the first to propose a different reading of Mauss,
to seize upon some of his observations that had hitherto been left
unanalyzed by his commentators, foremost among them Claude

Lévi-Strauss. Annette Weiner's book triggered my desire to return to my material on the Baruya and to rethink the facts.

But this stimulus would not have sufficed without the third context, that of the Western capitalist societies with their widening gulf between the economy and society, their growing appeals for gifts, for generosity to plug the gaps, the tears in the social fabric. Gift-giving is again becoming a social necessity where the economy excludes millions of people, at a time when earning money has become the general condition for one's material and social existence, where family and community solidarity have shrunk or broken down altogether, and where the individual is isolated within the society by society. Exclusion from the economy quite simply means potential exclusion from society as a whole. In an era where the idea that "Everything is for sale," as the title of Robert Kuttner's book says (New York: Knopf, 1997), is rapidly gaining worldwide credence, it is urgent that historians and anthropologists begin to reexamine the place of nonmarket relations in market societies, and to seek to determine whether there are realities essential to the life of societies that lie beyond the market and that will continue to do so.

These, then, are the three contexts that meshed and sparked my desire to reexplore the question of gift-giving and to reread Mauss. But a rereading of Mauss is not necessarily a return to Mauss, for we shall see that many of the facts reported in his book have not been analyzed, either by Mauss himself or by his commentators, and many of the questions he did raise have gone unanswered by himself first. But perhaps it would be helpful, at this point, to recall the climate in which Mauss wrote the *Essai sur le don*. It was immediately after the end of the First World War, in which Mauss had lost one-half of his friends. As a socialist, he had backed Jaurès, one of the leaders of the European socialist movement, who was assassinated for opposing the war. As a renowned academic, Mauss wrote a column for the popular weekly *L'Humanité*. Again as a socialist, he had made a postwar visit to Russia, where the communists were building their power structure, and had come back hostile to bolshevism for two reasons: because they wanted to construct an economy that bypassed the market, and because they made systematic use of violence to transform society. But Mauss was most critical, in his *Essai*, of liberalism, and he did not want society to become progressively imprisoned in what he called the "cold reasoning of the merchant, the banker, and the capitalist."

In 1921, fifteen years before the Front populaire swept to victory in France, he drew up a "social-democratic program" in which he asked the state to provide workers with material assistance and social protection. But he also appealed to the rich and the powerful to demonstrate the kind of self-interested generosity that was practiced by the Melanesian chiefs and the Kwakiutl noblemen, and that had formerly been exercised in Europe by the ancient Celtic and Germanic noblemen. Furthermore, he considered that even after centuries of Christianity, charity was "still wounding for him who has accepted it." So you see, there seems to be a continuity between our era of world economy and the era that inspired Mauss.

What is giving for Mauss? It is an act that creates a double relationship between donor and recipient. To give is to share, of one's own free will, what one has or what one is. An obligatory gift is not a gift. A gift freely given brings the giver closer to the receiver. But at the same time, the gift creates a debt, obligations for the receiver. Giving produces two things at once, then. It both reduces the distance and creates distance between the two parties. It creates a dissymmetry, a hierarchy between giver and receiver. Thus, from the outset, Mauss sets out the analytic principle that gift-giving cannot be studied in isolation; it is part of a set of relations between individuals and groups that arises from the concatenation of three obligations: the obligation to give, the obligation to accept the gift, and the obligation to reciprocate once one has accepted.

It was because he had defined the giving of a gift as the first link in a chain of acts whose structure must be analyzed as a whole that Lévi-Strauss celebrated Mauss as the precursor of structuralism, that is, as his own forerunner. But only a precursor, for, according to Lévi-Strauss, in the course of his *Essai,* Mauss had unfortunately lost sight of the methodological principles he had established at the outset, and had mistaken for a general scientific explanation of the obligation to reciprocate what was actually a particular indigenous explanation: old Tamati Ranaipiri's account to the anthropologist Elsdon Best of the Maori beliefs concerning the existence of a spirit (*hau*) in the thing given that compelled the receiver to give back the thing or something equivalent. In sum, for Lévi-Strauss, Mauss had allowed himself to be "mystified" by a subtle and complex indigenous ideology; this was not the first time an anthropologist had fallen into such a trap.

Indeed there was a flaw in Mauss's reasoning, and Lévi-Strauss lost no time in seizing upon it, proposing instead another explanation of the notions of hau or *mana,* which he interpreted as "signifiers in their pure state" or "floating signifiers." For Lévi-Strauss, when the human mind is confronted with something it cannot explain, it invents empty concepts that directly manifest the unconscious structures of the mind and at the same time attest to the symbolic origin of society. In short, the notions of mana, hau, and manitou demonstrate the primacy of language and, on a deeper level, the primacy of the symbolic over the imaginary and the real. For Lévi-Strauss, symbols are ultimately even more real than the reality they symbolize.

I personally think that if I had to assign primacy, I would say that it is the imaginary that dominates the symbolic rather than the converse. For sacred objects and valuables are first and foremost objects of belief; and their nature is imaginary before it is symbolic, because these beliefs concern the nature and the sources of power and wealth, whose content has always been, in part, imaginary. The shells exchanged for a woman or given to compensate the death of a warrior are symbolic substitutes for human beings, the imaginary equivalents of a life and of life.

But where, exactly, is the flaw in Mauss's theory? In explanation of the first two obligations, that of giving and that of accepting gifts, Mauss advances sociological reasons. One is obligated to give because giving creates obligations, and one is obligated to accept because to refuse a gift threatens to create a conflict with the giver. But when he comes to the third obligation, that of reciprocating, Mauss offers another type of explanation that relies primarily on ideological reasons and, in the case at hand, on mystical religious beliefs. What compels the receiver of a gift to reciprocate, he argues, is a force, the action of a "spirit" present in the thing received and that compels it to return to its original owner. Reading Mauss more closely, it would seem, moreover, that the thing given is inhabited by not one spirit but two. One is the spirit of the object's original owner, who gave it in the first place. But the thing itself seems to have a soul as well and, therefore, to exist as a person with the power to act on others. In short, by espousing these Maori beliefs, Mauss seems to be trying to indicate that the thing given is not completely alienated, that it remains attached to its owner and is, therefore, at the same time both inalienable and alienated. How can this duality be explained?

Lévi-Strauss appeals to the unconscious structures of the mind, Mauss to the religious representations of societies. Perhaps the explanation does not lie in either, but in the fact that the thing given is invested with two legal principles at the same time: an inalienable right of ownership and an alienable right of use. This very interpretation, as we shall see, is the one used by the Trobriand islanders themselves to explain the functioning of their ceremonial exchanges, the famous kula, which Mauss analyzed as the Melanesian counterpart of the American Indian potlatch. But Malinowski never discovered this explanation of the kula mechanism, and Mauss could not have known about it. We owe this discovery to Annette Weiner and to Frederick Damon, who began fieldwork in the 1960s in the Trobriand Islands and on Woodlark Island, respectively, two essential points in the kula-ring, that set of exchange routes that connects a series of islands and societies in the New Guinea Massim region.

Before going on, I want to repeat that Mauss was not interested in all forms of gift exchange. He was concerned with what he called "total prestations," those exchanges involving whole groups or persons acting as representatives of groups. Mauss was not interested in the gifts that a friend might make to a friend. Nor was he interested in the (imaginary) gift that a god might make of his life in order to save mankind. He was interested in gifts that are socially necessary for producing and reproducing social relationships—kinship relations, ritual relations—or the very conditions for social existence. As examples of these, he cites gifts of women between clans, rites performed by one moiety of a society for the benefit of the other, and so forth. Such prestations he qualifies as "total," a term he uses to designate two different things: either the fact that gift-giving has a number of dimensions (economic, political, religious, artistic—and, therefore, the act condenses many aspects of the society itself), or the fact that, by engendering a constant flow of countergifts, gift exchange mobilizes the wealth and energy of numerous groups and individuals, drawing the whole society into the movement and presenting itself as a mechanism and a moment that are essential to the reproduction of the society as a whole.

But Mauss emphasizes something we have forgotten: that there are two types of total prestation, one of which he calls "non-agonistic" and the other "agonistic." However, he says almost nothing about the logic of non-agonistic prestations, and his book privileges the analysis of agonistic gift exchange, which he designates in a general way by a term borrowed from the Chinook language: *potlatch.*

Mauss clearly indicates (something that is not usually mentioned) that the starting point of his analysis is non-agonistic gift exchange, but this departure point is not to be found in his *Essai.* Rather, we find it, for example, in his 1947 *Manuel d'ethnographie.* There he cites the examples of the exchange of goods, rituals, names, and so forth between the groups and individuals of the two moieties of dualist societies. He mentions in passing the names of several Australian or North American tribes, but without going into the particular logic of these gift exchanges. I will attempt to fill in this gap because, in the course of my fieldwork in New Guinea, I had the occasion to observe the exchange of women between the lineages and clans that make up the Baruya society in which I spent so many years.

You are all familiar with the basic principle: one lineage gives a woman to another lineage, a man gives one of his real or classificatory sisters to another man who, in turn, gives him one of his own real or classificatory sisters. To all appearances, these reciprocal gifts should cancel the debt each created. But this is not the case. When a lineage gives a woman to another lineage, it creates a debt in the receiving lineage and finds itself in a relationship of superiority with respect to it. But when the first lineage in turn receives a woman, it now becomes indebted and of inferior status. Finally, at the end of these reciprocal exchanges, each lineage finds itself both superior and inferior to the other. Both are, therefore, once more on an equal footing, since each is at the same time in a superior and an inferior position with regard to the other. Thus, countergifts do not cancel the debts created by gifts. They create new debts that counterbalance the earlier ones. According to this logic, the gifts constantly feed obligations, debts, thereby setting up a flow of services, mutual assistance and reciprocal obligations of solidarity. These debts are never canceled or extinguished in one fell swoop; instead, they gradually die out over time.

These examples show that to give in turn does not mean to repay, which is hard for a Western mind to grasp. They also show how absurd it would be for a man to give two women for the one he had received. The end result of such non-agonistic gift exchanges is a relatively egalitarian redistribution of the resources available to the groups that make up the society, resources in the form of human beings (women and children), goods, labor, and services. According to this logic, a woman equals a woman, the death of one warrior is compensated by that of another, and so on. The sphere of equivalences between objects and subjects, between material wealth and human beings—living or dead— remains restricted. It is no use amassing wealth to get women, or women to accumulate wealth. Accumulating wealth and women does not enhance your name, therefore your influence, and therefore your power. We now see why this type of gift-giving in New Guinea is often associated with Great Man societies rather than with Big Man societies. In the latter, as the work of Andrew Strathern, Darryl Feil, and many others has taught us, the fame of a Big Man and his group depends on their continued success in a cycle of competitive ceremonial exchanges such as the *moka,* the *tee,* and so forth.

The potlatch (and agonistic gift exchange in general), on the other hand, operates according to a totally different logic. Mauss emphasizes that the potlatch is a veritable "war of wealth" waged for the purpose of winning titles, ranks, and power, in which the spirit of competition dominates that of generosity. We are dealing, as he said, with another type of "economy and moral code dominated by gift-giving." Using descriptions taken from Boas and older Russian and Canadian authors, Mauss shows that potlatches were given in order to legitimize the transmission of a title that had already been acquired or to obtain the recognition of one's right to acquire it. The potlatch is therefore an exercise in power, which entails accumulating massive quantities of valuables and subsistence goods in order to redistribute them in the course of ceremonial feasting and competition. At the outset there are several competing clans and their chiefs, but at the finish line there is only one winner, at least for the time being, for as long as it takes another clan to mount a challenge with an even bigger potlatch. This is no longer the logic of non-agonistic gift exchanges that end in the relatively equal distribution of the resources necessary to the reproduction of the social groups involved.

Another difference is that a potlatch debt can be canceled by a countergift. A debt is canceled when a man gives more than he has received, and the ideal is for a clan ultimately to give so much that no one can reciprocate and that it stands alone, unrivaled. Once again we see that debt is an essential component of the logic of gift exchange. And in the potlatch, it is the very goal. But as a debt can be canceled by a greater countergift, which in turn creates a new debt, a whirlpool movement is set up that produces a relentless escalation of gifts and countergifts, thereby sucking the entire society into the spiral.

What I have given is a rough outline of Mauss's analysis of the potlatch. Nevertheless, in his text we find some facts that he has not investigated and that his commentators have not mentioned. For instance, in one footnote he states that the best Kwakiutl coppers, like their greatest titles, "do not go outside of the clans and tribes" and were never entered in potlatch. They were kept in the treasure of the clan, whereas the other coppers—the greater number—that circulated in the potlatches had less value and seemed to "serve as satellites for the first kind." Of all those who have commented this text, Annette Weiner is the only one to point out the importance of these observations, in her *Inalienable Possessions: The Paradox of Keeping-While-Giving* (1992). This point, which no one had seen as a problem, in fact alters the whole perspective on those things that can be given or sold, since it introduces the category of things that must neither be sold nor given, but that must be kept.

Before we analyze this category of objects, let us come back to Mauss's theories on the existence of a spirit in things, which presupposes the absence of any real distinction between things and persons. He suggests that this belief is characteristic of the social and mental worlds of many non-Western societies and that it is even the key to the ancient codes of law found in Greek and Latin antiquity, before the emergence of the distinction between personal law and real law, and in ancient Hindu and Chinese law. As we have seen, Mauss was trying to understand why a thing that has been given must be returned to the donor or must provoke the return of something equivalent. Already in 1921, while praising the richness of Malinowski's ethnographic material, Mauss regretted that it did not cast much light on the gifts and countergifts exchanged in the kula. He wrote:

> Sociologically, it is once again the mixture of things, values, contracts, and men that is so expressed. Unfortunately, our knowledge of the legal rule that governs these transactions is defective. It is either an unconscious rule, imperfectly formulated by the Kiriwina people, Malinowski's informants; or, if it is clear for the Trobriand people, it should be the subject of a fresh enquiry. We only possess details (Mauss 1923–24, 26).

It is not certain that Mauss believed it was clear for the Trobriand people, for he speaks of their confusing categories. But his formulation of the problem was prophetic. The answer, however, came only with a new series of research begun in the 1970s by Annette Weiner, Frederick Damon, Nancy Munn, Jerry Leach, John Liep, and others, and conducted in a dozen societies, all of which were part of the kula ring.

Their findings made us realize that the kula that Malinowski described as being practiced on Kiriwina was an exception and not the rule. On Kiriwina, only the nobles could engage in kula, and not the commoners, who were thus deprived of the means of raising their status by success in kula exchanges.

This is not the case in other kula-ring societies. But let us look once more at the way kula is conducted. The practice is to send an armband into circulation in the hope of obtaining in exchange a necklace of the same rank, or vice versa. Note that in this game, it is never the same object or kind of object that takes the place of the one given. It is, therefore, impossible to argue that a spirit present in the thing compels the receiver of the gift to give it back to the original owner. Mauss regretted this, writing:

Malinowski has not found any mythical or other reasons for the direction of this circulation of the vaygu'a [that is, the valuables that circulate in the kula]. It would be very important to discover them. For if there was any reason for the orientation of these objects, so that they tended to return to their point of origin . . . the fact would be miraculously identical to . . . the Maori *hau* (Mauss 1923–24, 102 n. 32).

Unfortunately, that is not what was found. Malinowski had missed two key indigenous concepts that illuminate the kula exchanges and explain why the owner appears to remain present in the object, even after it has been given. These two concepts are kitoum and keda. What is a kitoum? These are things owned by a lineage or even an individual: canoes, shells, stone ax blades, and the like. As kitoum, they can be used by their owners in various contexts and for different purposes. They can be used as compensation for the killing of an enemy, or as bridewealth, to obtain a wife; they can be exchanged for a large canoe, or sold to an American tourist, and so forth. But they can also be launched on a kula exchange path, a keda. Once a necklace is sent along a kula path and has left its owner's hands and come into the possession of the first recipient, it becomes a *vaygu'a,* an object that can no longer be used for any purpose other than kula exchanges. It continues to belong to the original giver, who can ask the temporary possessor to give it back, thus taking it out of kula. This practically never happens, but the fact that it is theoretically possible clearly indicates the relationship between the original donor and the object he has given. What he cedes when he gives the object is not its ownership, but the right to use it for making other gifts. None of those through whose hands the object will pass may use it as a kitoum and thus give it to compensate a killing or to procure a wife. And yet the object given may never return to its original owner, for what comes back in place of a necklace is an armband of equivalent rank, which has been ceded by someone who owned it and wanted to exchange it for a necklace. The armband then travels back along the chain of intermediaries until it finally reaches the necklace owner, who will appropriate it as a kitoum, which closes that particular exchange path (keda).

So there is, indeed, a legal rule that explains how valuables circulating in gift exchanges can be alienated and still be the inalienable property of their original donor. What this rule does not explain is why it applies to valuables but not to sacred objects, which are often of the same nature as the valuables: rare shells or very old coppers, for example. And yet, like sacred objects, valuables are endowed with an imaginary value not to be confused with the labor invested in locating or manufacturing them, nor with their relative rareness. This imaginary value reflects the fact that they can be exchanged for a life, that they are made equivalent to human beings. The time has come, therefore, to cross the line that Mauss did not cross.

But before I make this step, I will conclude my analysis of the potlatch and other forms of agonistic gift exchanges by proposing the following hypothesis, which Mauss did not suggest, namely that such forms of competition emerge historically only if two sociological and ideological conditions are present and associated. In the first place, marriage must no longer be based, for the most part, on the direct exchange of women; this practice must have yielded to the generalized use of bridewealth, that is, the exchange of wealth for women. And in the second place, some of the positions of power and prestige characteristic of a society and, therefore, part of its political field, must be accessible through the redistribution, in the form of ceremonial gift exchanges, of wealth accumulated by the competing groups and individuals. When these two types of social relationships are combined within the same society, it seems that the conditions are present for the emergence of potlatch practices. Moreover, potlatch societies are not as numerous as Mauss imagined. He saw this as a widespread transitional economic system situated between primitive societies practicing non-agonistic gift exchange and market societies. To be sure, today we know of many more examples of ceremonial gift exchange than did Mauss—for example, in New Guinea, Asia, and so forth—but the number is still low and cannot be compared with the much more frequent presence of non-agonistic giving of gifts and countergifts.

Which brings us to the things that must not be sold or given, but that must be kept—for example, sacred objects. These are often presented as gifts, but gifts that the gods or the spirits are supposed to have given to the ancestors of men, and that their present-day descendants must keep safely stored away and neither sell nor give. Consequently, they are presented and experienced as an essential component of the identities of the groups and the individuals who have received them into their care. These groups and individuals may use them on their own behalf, or for the benefit of all other members of the society. But they can also use them to inflict harm. Sacred objects are thus a source of power within and over society and, unlike valuables, they are presented as being both inalienable and unalienated.

My fieldwork in New Guinea gave me numerous occasions to see the uses to which a sacred object might be put. Among the Baruya, a certain number of clans own kwaimatnie. These are bundles containing objects that are never seen and that are wrapped in strips of red-colored bark, the color of the sun. The Baruya call themselves the "sons of the sun." The word *kwaimatnie* comes from *kwala,* "men," and *nimatnie,* "to cause to grow." The kwaimatnie are kept in a secret place in the house of the masters of the boys' initiations. These masters represent the clans responsible for the different stages of the initiation, which takes place over a period of more than ten years and ends with the boys' marriage. Around the age of nine, the boys are torn away from their mothers and the world of women, and shut away in the men's house at the top of the village. There they are introduced to various sacred objects: flutes, bull-roarers, and kwaimatnie. Later they learn that the flutes were originally owned by the women, and that an ancestor of the men stole them. These flutes contained, and still contain, the powers women have to make children, even without men. Just what is inside a kwaimatnie? I had the honor and the joy of having an initiation master one day show me the contents of his. I saw, wrapped in strips of bark, a black stone and a pointed bone from an eagle, the sun's bird. The man said nothing, but I knew, from having been partially initiated myself, that for the Baruya, the stone contained something of the powers of the "star" Venus. For them, Venus is the metamorphosis of a woman given by their dream-time ancestors to propitiate the serpent Python, god of rain and master of thunder. The bull-roarers are said to be objects that the Yimaka, forest spirits, formerly gave an ancestor of the Baruya and that are supposed to contain powers of death: the power to kill game or enemy warriors.

Thus in the sacred objects, which only a few men may touch or handle and which are the exclusive property of certain clans, are conjoined two types of powers: women's powers, powers of life that men are supposed (imaginarily) to have expropriated; and men's powers, those of death and war received directly from the forest spirits. But in the eyes of the Baruya, women still own the powers of which they were dispossessed by men, even if they are no longer able to use them. This is why men must resort to violence in order to separate the boys from the women's world, and initiate them into the secrets of these powers they have appropriated from women. Baruya men justify this expropriation by telling how the first women did not use their powers for the good of society. They killed too much game, for instance, and caused many kinds of disorder. The men had to intervene and dispossess them of their powers so that society and the cosmos might be restored to order.

Last of all, a sacred object is a material object that represents the unrepresentable, which refers men back to the origin of things and attests to the legitimacy of the cosmic and social order that replaced the primal time and its events. A sacred object does not have to be beautiful. A splinter of the "true Cross" is more than beautiful, it is sublime. A sacred object places men in the presence of the forces that command the invisible order of the world. For those who handle and exhibit them, sacred objects are not symbols. They are experienced and thought of as the real presence of forces that are the source of the powers that reside in them.

It is important, moreover, to note that in the stories relating the circumstances in which a particular object was given to the mythic ancestors of today's real men and women, these ancestors appear as both larger and smaller than their descendants. Larger because they were capable of communicating constantly and *directly* with the gods and of receiving gifts from their hands; smaller as well, because these first men did not yet know how to do the things done by people today—hunt, work the land, marry, initiate their children. They received everything from the gods. The sacred object, then, is a "material" synthesis of the imaginary and symbolic components present in the relations that organize real societies. The interests at stake in the imaginary and the symbolic always have a real social impact. For instance, when the rites have been performed, and in the name of their myths, Baruya women are really, and not merely symbolically or imaginarily, dispossessed of land ownership, the use of weapons, and access to the gods.

In this perspective, one might postulate that the monopoly of sacred objects, rites, and other imaginary means of access to the forces that control the cosmos and society must have preceded the development of various forms of exclusive control of the material conditions of social existence and production of wealth, namely the land and its resources, or individuals and their labor. And one might cite the example of the Australian aboriginal rites for multiplying the living species, and the monopoly of initiated men on the sacred objects, the *tjuringas*.

I am not saying that religion is the source of the caste or class relations that have grown up in many parts of the world since neolithic times. But it does seem that religion may have supplied ready-made models for representing and legitimizing the new forms of power in places where certain social groups and their representatives were beginning to raise themselves well above the others. They were desirous of legitimizing their place in this now-different society in a new way. Did not the Inca present himself as the son of the sun? And pharaoh as a god dwelling among men?

To get to the bottom of the nature of sacred objects, we would need to go even further and understand that they are an ultimate testimonial to the opacity necessary for the production and reproduction of societies. In the sacred object, the men who manufactured it are at once present and absent: they are present, but in a form such that it dissimulates the fact that men themselves are at the origin of the forces that dominate them and that they worship. This is the very same relationship men have with money when it functions as capital, as money that makes money, thereby appearing capable of reproducing itself unaided, of generating money independently of the men who produced it.

It is not true, then, even in highly developed capitalist societies, that "Everything is for sale." Let us take the example of the constitution of a Western democracy. It is a fact that votes can be and frequently are bought in democratic societies, but it is not yet possible to run down to the supermarket and buy a constitution.

Democracy signifies that each person, however rich or poor, whatever the gender or social function, possesses an equal share of political sovereignty. To be sure, a democratic constitution is not a code of law given by God. It is a set of principles that people give to themselves as a means of organizing their life together and that they oblige themselves to respect. A democratic constitution is a common good that, by its very essence, is not the product of market relations but of political relations and negotiation. For this reason, in a democracy the political power of each person is an inalienable possession.

But let us go a step further. The expansion of the market has its limits, and some of these are absolute. Can one imagine, for instance, a child making a contract with its parents to be born? The very idea is absurd, and its absurdity demonstrates that the first bond among humans, namely birth, is not negotiated between the parties concerned. From its inception, life is established as a gift and a debt, in whatever society this new life may appear.

In conclusion, I would like to present a sort of general hypothesis concerning the conditions of existence and production of human societies. For people not only live in society, like the other primates and social animals, they also produce society in order to live. And it seems to me that, in order to produce society, three bases and three principles must be combined. There must be certain things that are given, others that are sold or bartered, and still others that must be kept for good. In our societies, buying and selling have become the main activity. Selling means completely separating the thing from the person. Giving means maintaining something of the person in the thing given. And keeping means not separating the thing from the person, because in this union resides the affirmation of a historical identity that must be passed on, at least until that time when it can no longer be reproduced. It is because these three operations—selling, giving, and keeping—are not the same that objects in these contexts are presented respectively as alienable and alienated (commodities), as inalienable but alienated (gift objects), and inalienable and unalienated (sacred objects).

Finally, by going back to Boas, Malinowsky, and Mauss, and working forward to Annette Weiner, Fred Damon, Andrew Strathern, and many others, we have completed a circuit that shows that, naysayers notwithstanding, anthropology has constantly shown itself capable of gathering new knowledge about people, their ways of thinking and acting, even if we do not formulate this knowledge in the same terms as the actors themselves. But at the same time, it is no use trying to shut one's eyes to the fact that in every society, men and women find many ways and reasons to avoid seeing or recognizing themselves in what they do. Whence the important critical function of anthropology and the social sciences. Our task as anthropologists is precisely to attempt, in conjunction with these other disciplines, to seek out man where he is at the origin of himself.

Translated by Nora Scott

BIBLIOGRAPHY

Damon, Frederick. 1993. "Representation and Experience in Kula and Western Exchange Epheres (Or, Billy)." *Research in Economic Anthropology* 14: 235–54.

———. 1980. "The Kula and Generalized Exchange: Considering Some Unconsidered Aspects of the Elementary Structures of Kinship." *Man* 15, no. 2: 267–92.

Feil, Daryl Keith. 1984. *Ways of Exchange: The Enga Tee of Papua New Guinea*. St. Lucia, Queensland: University of Queensland Press.

———. 1981. "The Bride in Bridewealth: A Case from the New Guinea Highlands." *Ethnology* 20, no. 1: 63–75.

Fournier, Marcel. 1995. *Marcel Mauss*. Paris: Fayard.

———. 1995. "Marcel Mauss, L'ethnologue et la politique: Le don." *Anthropologie et sociétés* 19, no. 1–2: 57–69.

Godelier, Maurice. 1984. *L'idéel et le matériel*. Paris: Fayard.

———. 1982. *La production des grands hommes*. Paris: Fayard.

———. 1966. *Rationalité et irrationalité en économie*. Paris: Maspero.

Godelier, Maurice, and Marilyn Strathern, eds. 1991. *Big Men and Great Men: Personifications of Power in Melanesia*. Cambridge: Cambridge University Press.

Leach, Jerry, and Edmound Leach, eds. 1983. *The Kula: New Perspectives on Massim Exchange*. Cambridge: Cambridge University Press.

Lévi-Strauss, Claude. 1950. "Introduction à l'oeuvre de Mauss," in Marcel Mauss, *Sociologie et anthropologie.* Paris: PUF.

Malinowski, Bronislaw. 1922. *Argaunauts of the Western Pacific.* London: Routledge.

———. 1921. "The Primitive Economics of the Trobriand Islanders." *Economic Journal* 31, no. 121 (March): 1–16.

Mauss, Marcel. 1950. *Sociologie et anthropologie.* Paris: PUF.

———. 1947. *Manuel d'ethnographie.* Paris: Payot.

———. 1923–24. "Essai sur le don: Forme et raison de l'échange dans les sociétés archaïques," *L'année sociologique,* new series 1.

———. 1914. "Origine de la notion de monnaie." *Anthropologie* (revue de l'Institut français d'anthropologie) 3, no. 1: 14–20.

Mauss, Marcel, and Henri Hubert. 1898. "Essai sur la nature et la fonction du sacrifice." *L'année sociologique,* 29–138.

Sahlins, Marshall. 1970. "The Spirit of the Gift: Une explication de texte," in *Échanges et communications,* mélanges offerts à Claude Lévi-Strauss à l'occasion de son 60e anniversaire. Leiden: Mouton.

———. 1965. "On the Sociology of Primitive Exchange," in Michael Banton, ed., *The Relevance of Models for Social Anthropology.* London: Tavistock Publication.

———. 1963. "Poor Man, Rich Man, Big Man, Chief," *Comparative Studies in Society and History* 5, no. 3: 285–303.

Strathern, Andrew. 1983. "The *Kula* in Comparative Perspective," in Jerry Leach and Edmund Leach, eds., *The Kula: New Perspectives on Massim Exchange.* Cambridge: Cambridge University Press.

———. 1980. "The Central and the Contingent: Bridewealth among the Melpa and the Wiru," in J. L. Komaroff, ed., *The Meaning of Marriage Payments.* London: Academic Press.

———. 1978. "Finance and Production Revisited," in G. Dalton, ed., *Research in Economic Anthropology.* Greenwich, Conn.: J.A.I. Press.

———. 1978. "Tambu and Kina: 'Profit,' Exploitation and Reciprocity in Two New Guinea Exchange Systems." *Mankind* 11, no. 3: 253–64.

———. 1971. *The Rope of Moka: Big Men and Ceremonial Exchange in Mount-Hagen, New Guinea.* Cambridge: Cambridge University Press.

———. 1969. "Finance and Production: Two Strategies in New Guinea Exchange Systems." *Oceania* 40, no. 1: 42–67.

Weiner, Annette. 1992. *Inalienable Possessions: The Paradox of Keeping-While-Giving.* Berkeley and Los Angeles: University of California Press.

———. 1985. "Inalienable Wealth." *American Ethnologist* 12, no. 2: 210–27.

———. 1976. *Women of Value, Men of Renown: New Perspectives in Trobriand Exchange.* Austin: University of Texas Press.

Weiner, Annette, and Jane Schneider. 1989. *Cloth and Human Experience.* Washington, D.C.: Smithsonian Institution Press.

2

The Gift and Globalization: A Prolegomenon to the Anthropological Study of Contemporary Finance Capital and Its Mentalities

George E. Marcus

THIS PAPER explores a recent collective interest among the anthropologists at Rice University concerning forms of circulation—of things, of peoples, of techniques, of meanings, of discourses—as themselves cultural objects of analysis. This is much stimulated by the changing empirical character of culture itself, at least as it has been constituted for ethnographic study in anthropology. The phenomena that anthropologists have studied as situated, as located in distinctive places—such as rituals, kinship systems, norms of community, political processes, and the like—now seem to be themselves more in motion or to be defined more systematically by processes for which metaphors of continual movement such as flow and circulation seem apt. Of course societies and cultures have always been in motion, but there is something about the characteristics of their circulation (techniques, media, and, indeed, culture in different spheres) that makes the reigning fictions of the real in anthropology, in the form of geoculture areas of historically rooted peoples and places, less serviceable for the project of ethnography. And it is not just anthropology that is feeling this need to reconstitute the spatial and temporal frames by which it materializes its objects of study. This predicament is shared as well by all those disciplines and journalists who label the monster of the present as globalization, perhaps the leading common trope of this millennial transition to refer to what we cannot fully understand but that demands representation anyhow.

The challenge for anthropology is to devise a research program that can lend meaning, precision, and "a native's point of view" to this rather abstract construct of processes known as globalization: to harness it, by ethnographic methods of study, as a cultural object of analysis. And this does not mean merely refocusing upon the peoples that ethnography has traditionally and comfortably studied and following them in their diasporic and exilic movements to new places and local situations, but to study the engines and forces of political economy and technology that stimulate such movements as well. What is needed, then, is a general sense of circulation itself—not as the pathways, tracks, or traces of objects and subjects that can indeed, as ever, be studied ethnographically, but as a form of culture. What is the sort of research imaginary required to understand circulation as an object of study? What sorts of adaptations in the method of participant observation and the ethnographic principle of understanding worlds through native points of view are necessary to study circulations?

These kinds of questions are worthy successors to the critique that was delivered to traditional ethnographic authority in the 1980s by the volume *Writing Culture* (Clifford and Marcus 1986). While not irrelevant to this second wave of critical thought that I am suggesting, this time the critique focuses more broadly on the conditions of the production of anthropological knowledge—the imaginaries of ethnographic fieldwork itself—it is not so much the textual form that ethnography takes that is the problem now, but what is conceived as its object of study, and whether the idea of culture, or even society, can continue to lend coherence to this object. I believe that the earlier concern with the written form of the ethnography invaluably offers resources for experimental thinking about this distinctively 1990s problem—that the seemingly shapeless, the ephemeral, or the ever-changing can be taken as something that can be investigated by the norms of fieldwork, insofar as this shapelessness manifests itself as culture, as language, as behavior, and as human.

The experimental lab for addressing such questions of the culture of circulation is in the realm of the hard or extreme cases: where what is studied has long been impervious to cultural analysis. This might, for instance, be the realm of the economic, of political economy, of money, of finance capitalism, of intellectual property that has been so much in the news of late as, if not the engine of globalization, then its key source of perturbation.

To begin thinking about an anthropology of the form of the processes at the heart of globalization, there are ironic originary sources of anthropology's own to fall back upon. If there is one body of theory that modern anthropology made its own and used as the very foundation of the study of traditional societies and of all of the topics for which anthropology is famous for developing—kinship, ritual, myth—it is that of exchange. And the primary source of the theory that has been the object of generations of rich and complex theorization in anthropology from Lévi-Strauss to Pierre Bourdieu, Marshall Sahlins, Annette Weiner, Marilyn Strathern, Jacques Derrida, and, of course, Maurice Godelier, is Marcel Mauss's essay on the gift and the works and commentaries around it in interwar French anthropology. But it is not only for anthropology and culture theory in general that this essay has been such a beacon: it has found its way, frequently and improbably, into the genealogy of references of writers such as George Gilder and George Soros, among others. These figures have attempted to write new theologies or gospels of wealth (following upon Andrew Carnegie's famous 1889 essay) explicating the ways in which capitalism has developed in the postmodern 1980s and 1990s.

For the purpose of considering the possibility of an anthropology of the culture of circulation in the sphere of finance capitalism as satisfying as its study of traditional societies, I want to address from this vast literature two key revisions of Mauss that might help this project—that of Bourdieu, which for the first time changes the terms through which Mauss was received by the main structuralist channel of Lévi-Strauss; and that of Georges Bataille, a student and contemporary of Mauss, who fashioned a discourse on the gift relevant to modern capitalism.

In the opening pages of his classic *Outline of a Theory of Practice*

(1966), Pierre Bourdieu displaces the predominant structuralist appropriation of *The Gift* and reinstantiates more powerfully the phenomenological understanding of exchange that Lévi-Strauss claimed that Mauss had originally given it. In so doing, Bourdieu opens the basic terms of acts of giving and receiving to questions of experience, strategy, and misrecognition. Most importantly, he emphasizes the situated perception and manipulation of temporalities as what must be given priority in the analysis of exchange. And he removes the weight of moral prescription and rules as the factors that are most defining of the gift, or any form of exchange. As he says: "In short, everything takes place as if agents' practice, and in particular their manipulation of *time*, were organized exclusively with a view to concealing from themselves and from others the truth by substituting the timeless model for a scheme which works itself out only in and through time" (Bourdieu 1966, 3–4).

Bourdieu thus modernizes the Maussian understanding of the gift at the level of the structure of feeling, to evoke Raymond Williams (1976), and he replaces "political man" with "moral man" in which meaning is only rarely transparent and is produced by the management of time. This lays the basis for considering exchange or circulation itself as a regime of culture. And, outside the realm of traditional societies, with their redundant monitoring of transactions, it normalizes paranoia within the practice of rational calculation as the prime imaginary or structure of feeling for cultures of circulation (see Marcus 1998). While Bourdieu is even still writing about the Kabyle of Algeria, a traditional people, he is nonetheless doing so at the height of the Cold War and in the era of postcolonization, both of which leave their marks on his style of sociology where game, field, strategy, and maneuver define the habitus of actors.

Bourdieu, perhaps unreflexively, prepares the way for grasping native points of view in thoroughly modern—moving into post-modern—forms of capitalist circulation by his investing homologously in the Cold War professional craft of paranoid social science. Mauss's account of the gift's legacy in his era of bourgeois capitalism is far too optimistic and, indeed, nostalgic about how certain characteristics of his times might still be seen as, or developed in terms of, the gift's moral order. He, in his own context of writing, is an improbable reference for a theology of today's consumer—finance and fast capitalism—even though he is incorporated as part of such a scripture. Bourdieu, writing in the context of Cold War–game theorizing sociology, makes the temporalizing ambiguities and manipulations of exchange a much more usable way of delving into the riches of the minimalist cultures of circulation that organize so much of our social life.

Next I want to turn to a second key revision of Mauss: that by his student Georges Bataille, who suggests the possibility of cultures of circulation as an object of ethnographic study. Simply, instead of the impulse to give, posited by Mauss, there is the impulse to spend leading to scenarios and dramas of sacrifice, like the potlatch of Northwest coast tribes, rather than controlled, heavily moralized, and restricted regimes of exchange, like the Trobriand *kula* ring described by Malinowski (1928). An essential source here is Jean-Joseph Goux's fascinating essay (1990) on the appropriation of Bataille's Maussian revision by contemporary theologians of wealth in the regime of 1980s Reaganite style market capitalism. Combined with the phenomenology of time in exchange as emphasized by Bourdieu, the impulse to spend implies the mise-en-scène of risk, speculation, and impersonality that characterizes so much of the experience of exchange, especially given the quantum innovations in information technology available on a mass basis that have increased the quantity and salience of virtual relationships of all kinds. Little of the original Maussian phenomenology applies to exchanges within relationships of virtual time-space. Bataille's general economics are better and bolder. His direct assault on the utility-function, rationalist model of economics is inspirational for anyone who would give a cultural account of that which is thought to reduce life to calculation, to the value of the close-ended reflexivity of the general equivalent.

Goux raises the key problems with Bataille's redolent vision of *la part maudite* in modern capitalism, imagined by him primarily in terms of the extravagant expenditures of sumptuary wealth in premodern societies.

Productive expenditure now entirely dominates social life. In a de-sacralized world, where human labor is guided in the short or long term by the imperative of utility, the surplus has lost its meaning of glorious consumption and becomes capital to be reinvested pro-ductively, a constantly multiplying surplus-value. What happens to the demand of the sacred in capitalist society? How do we reconcile the affirmation that capitalism represents an unprecedented break with all archaic forms of expenditure and the postulate of the nec-essary universality of spending as pure loss? This is the difficulty. Bataille wants to maintain as a general anthropological principle the necessity of unproductive expenditure while simultaneously upholding the historic singularity of capitalism with regard to this expenditure. Bataille insists, "Today, the great and free social forms of unproductive expenditure have disappeared. Neverthe-less, we should not conclude from this that the very principle of expenditure is no longer situated at the end of economic activity" (Goux 1990, 76).

Well, can we make anything of this, ethnographically, today? Does the notion of spending to excess help in making regimes of circulation cultural objects of study? Certainly it would appear so, given unprecedented accumulations of wealth and resulting inequalities, and the hyperconcern of broad-based middle classes with expenditure as consumption, investment, and speculations. The invention of the credit card and the mutual fund, combined with internet transaction, has produced the worries and preroga-tives of wealth as middle-class norms.

Reflecting on the atmosphere of finance capitalism of the 1980s, Goux provides an acute commentary on the influential book of that period by George Gilder, *Wealth and Poverty* (New York: Basic Books, 1981). In order to distance the present from the narrow utilitarian form of bourgeois entrepreneurial capital-ism, Gilder makes lavish and ironic use of Mauss and Bataille. As a preface to postmodern capitalism, he overturns the classic assumptions of political economy, insisting instead that supply creates demand. As Goux says: "For what is remarkable is that Gilder is obliged to resort to the notion of gift and sacrifice at the moment when he is giving capitalism a noble and glorious image, an adventurous legitimation that goes beyond the secular ratio-nalist mentality" (1990, 81).

But what of the contemporary scene? Finance capitalism is in full flower. The shifts of capital are faster, vaster in scale, more profound in consequences, and with ripple effects. Bataillean-scale spending is the concern of both the individual and great collective projects at the same time. The prophetic role is less that of the visionary of wealth, as Gilder was in the 1980s, but is embedded in visionary circuits, connections, and investment habits. Now the theology of capitalism has many writers: the industry of corporate culture gurus and consultants, the technocapitalist prophecies of Bill Gates, and so on. In terms of the impulse to spend—that which drives exchange—perhaps the key contemporary writer is George Soros, who investigates the forms of investment and finance that generate cultures of circulation. George Soros, one of the most famous speculators of our times, who interestingly speculates both financially and intellectually, calls the state of affairs of the market its "reflexivity." In his most recent book, *The Crisis of Global Capitalism* (1998), he explores some of those risks and is very clear in his assessment of the danger of what he calls "market fundamentalism," the tendency to reduce all values to market values. These values can be determined with accuracy, the famous bottom line. Other values are, for instance, social values, which cannot easily, if at all, be subsumed under bottom-line calculations. They cannot be reduced to a common-denominator money. As Soros says:

> As an anonymous participant in financial markets, I never had to weigh the social consequences of my actions. I was aware that in some circumstances the consequences might be harmful but I felt justified in ignoring them on the grounds that I was playing by the rules. The game was very competitive and if I imposed additional constraints on myself I would wind up as a loser. Moreover, I realize that my moral scruples would make no difference to the real world, given the conditions of effective or near-perfect competition that prevail in financial markets; if I abstained somebody else would take my place. In deciding which stocks or currencies to buy or sell, I was guided by one consideration: to maximize my profits weighting the risks against the rewards . . . When I sold sterling short in 1992, the Bank of England was on the other side of my transactions and I was taking money out of the pockets of British taxpayers. But if I had tried to take the social consequences into account, it would

have thrown off my risk/reward calculations and my chances of being successful would have been reduced (1998, 196).

There is no better account of the contemporary expression of dispense than this, in which circulation is sovereign and yet is seen in all of its ramifications. There are, of course, other, even compensatory circuits—such as Soros's well known philanthropic interventions in eastern Europe and the former Soviet Union— but the realm of expenditure within its very tight sphere of invest- ment and finance cannot be disturbed by social considerations. What is it, then, that shapes this regime of circulation as a culture?

To begin to address this question, it is important for anthropol- ogy within contemporary "financescapes," as Arjun Appadurai (1997) has termed them, to inquire, below the level of highly public nabobs such as Soros, what spiritually or at least personally fuels present-day "masters of the world," the rank and file, so to speak, whose profession is to spend. Access to such voices and points of view has been at least partly available to us through the work of the Late Editions project, a series of annuals produced by the anthropology department at Rice University since the begin- ning of the 1990s and published by the University of Chicago Press (Marcus 1992–2000). While not actually being a project of ethnography, this series has been inspired by this method, as it has experimented with the situated ethnographic interview or conversation as a form of documentation in an era when the ex- pository, authoritative voice-over of documentary representation, in general, has been so thoroughly critiqued.

In particular, we have wanted to probe the social thought em- bedded in the uncertainties of subjects affected by a fin-de-siècle ethos. In the phrasing of Douglas Holmes (1992), who studies the nature of right-wing political thought in contemporary Europe, we have been exposing in this project the content and circulation of "illicit discourses." The discourse of dispense is a prominent variety of these in its various manifestations. We have produced assemblages of interviews and conversations under such topics as technoscience, corporations, disintegrating political orders, the emergence of virtual electronic communication, and the preva- lence of paranoia within hyperrational modes of thought. The series ends with Late Editions 8, *Zeroing in on the Year 2000* (Mar-

cus 2000), including, appropriately, a group of pieces on the
value of zero. In this final volume, for example, appears a piece
by Gudrun Klein (2000) which probes personal sentiment in the
frame of market fundamentalism. She shows that the most glorious forms of expenditure now are generated in a regime of circulation and exchange dominated by the rigid minimalism of zero.
A former academic herself, now in financial advising, she interviews a top executive of an investment company. This top executive is a member of the 1 percent of the population that owns 40
percent of U.S. assets, a former academic, now a "master of the
world"—in 1990s rather than 1980s style, as given by Tom Wolfe's
satiric formulation. We can listen a little into this conversation
here:

Q: What is money for you?

A: Money is freedom. The fact of the matter is in a capitalist
society freedom is largely determined by how much money you
have. There are exceptions to that. But certain exceptions, like
being bright, are tricky because the brighter you are, the more you
realize how little freedom you actually have without money. In
Western society, you can commit double murder and have all kinds
of evidence against you, and if you have money, you can have freedom. The criminal justice system, for instance, in America applies
differently to those who have money, as a practical matter. Money
means freedom and freedom means power, it seems to me. There
is a pretty close correlation between the amount of money you have
and the expectations you have about life and the amount of freedom that goes with it.

Q: Freedom is a value, it is also a state of mind, a way of living—
can you qualify that some more?

A: People place value on freedom because they want to be able
to be free. So they place value in money. So it seems to me that
both are currencies of the same realm. I don't think you can have
freedom without money. Not in the way these societies are structured.

Q: If you think of enslaved people, for instance, two hundred or
one hundred years ago in this country, what might freedom have
meant then versus now in your mind?

A: I think there are more similarities than differences between
then and now. Emancipation was available to slaves who could buy
their way from their owners. Manumission. And it happened time

and again. Indeed, it's a very stark example and puts into great relief how money means freedom in that context. I don't think that it's much different today. I believe that there are whole classes of people who are essentially slaves today. They are not slaves in the eighteenth/nineteenth century sense, but every bit as much in bondage. . . . If you define slavery to mean what I think it really means, which is that you basically are without opportunity and your life has no value, then you are in a large group of people to whom that applies.

Q: How does enjoying what you do in your work relate to the goal to make money?

A: There is a close correlation. It seems to me there are three ways to make money in Western society: There's the old-fashioned way, that is, to inherit. I encourage you to get the view on money from those folks because their view has to be interesting and different than mine. I have an extremely low regard for that crowd. And the reason I do is probably because I'm not a member of the lucky sperm club and they've just been gifted, literally, with this freedom which they have evidenced no entitlement to, other than being born to somebody, which to me is no entitlement. The second one is stealing. That's time-honored in Western society. There are different degrees. There's the person who holds up the convenience store. But they're not really getting money, real money, a large amount of money.

Q: Where does a large amount of money start?

A: The better question would be, where does freedom start? And that depends on your own self-image. I'm sure that for some people, freedom starts with thirty thousand dollars a year. For me, it doesn't. For me the question is, where is there freedom in terms of money? I guess rather than giving you a number, the concept would be that you'd be able to do whatever it is you wanted to do for the rest of your life without depending on dispensation of anyone else. . . . The third way of making money is what Western society is all about in a way. That is, through your wits and guile and smarts and tenacity you fashion a way and in so doing you reach a kind of "nirvana." Because what happens is you work harder than everybody else does but you don't think it is a job. And in fact you create jobs for other people and opportunity and so on. And that's what distinguishes that third way from others.

Q: So, how much money do you need to feel free?

A: [After some deliberation] There is always more freedom to have (Klein 2000, 195–97).

Freedom here is like money: it is spiritual and potentially infinite, but it is closely tied in a minimalist way to zero, to nothing, at the core of the general equivalent. This shows how difficult it is to evoke a discourse of social commitment around market fundamentalism. It is thus better to seek resources elsewhere for the proposal to understand circulation itself as a culture, perhaps toward a cultural history of the forms of circulation that shape what Bourdieu would call the habitus of actors like Soros or Klein's interlocutor. This requires us to know much more about the technical regimes of markets as cultural doctrines. Here, one might say, the *hau* or spirit of the gift evoked by the Maori elder Tamiti Ranaipiri to the anthropologist Elsdon Best in the early twentieth century, and of such interest to Mauss and later to writers such as Marshall Sahlins and Annette Weiner, is indeed the forms of circulation themselves—techniques such as derivatives, in their care, spread, appropriation, and regulation. Finally, just as traditional exchanges are constituted by this spirit or hau, so are the technical forms that define a contemporary culture of circulation.

BIBLIOGRAPHY

Appadurai, Arjun. 1997. *Modernity at Large.* Minneapolis: University of Minnesota Press.

Bourdieu, Pierre. 1966. *Outline of a Theory of Practice.* Cambridge: Cambridge University Press.

Carnegie, Andrew. 1889. "The Gospel of Wealth." *North American Review* 148: 653–64; 149: 682–98.

Clifford, James, and George E. Marcus, eds. 1986. *Writing Culture: The Poetics and Politics of Ethnography.* Berkeley and Los Angeles: University of California Press.

Goux, Jean-Joseph. 1990. "General Economics and Postmodern Capitalism," in Allan Stoekl, ed., *On Bataille.* Yale French Studies No. 78. New Haven: Yale University Press.

Holmes, Douglas. 1992. "Illicit Discourse," in George E. Marcus, ed., *Perilous States.* Late Editions 1. Chicago: University of Chicago Press.

Klein, Gudrun. 2000. "Zero/Money Matters," in George E. Marcus, ed., *Zeroing in on the Year 2000.* Late Editions 8. Chicago: University of Chicago Press.

Malinowski, Bronislaw. 1928. *Argonauts of the Western Pacific.* New York: Dutton.

Marcus, George E., ed. 1992. *Perilous States,* Late Editions 1. Chicago: University of Chicago Press.

————. 1993. *Technoscientific Imaginaries,* Late Editions 2. Chicago: University of Chicago Press.

————. 1994. *Connected,* Late Editions 3. Chicago: University of Chicago Press.

————. 1995. *Cultural Producers in Perilous States,* Late Editions 4. Chicago: University of Chicago Press.

————. 1996. *Corporate Futures,* Late Editions 5. Chicago: University of Chicago Press.

————. 1998. *Paranoia within Reason,* Late Editions 6. Chicago: University of Chicago Press.

————. 1999. *Para-sites,* Late Editions 7. Chicago: University of Chicago Press.

————. 2000. *Zeroing in on the Year 2000,* Late Editions 8. Chicago: University of Chicago Press.

Mauss, Marcel. 1990. *The Gift: The Form and Reason for Exchange in Archaic Societies.* Trans. W. D. Halls. New York: Norton.

Soros, George. 1998. *The Crisis of Global Capitalism.* New York: Public Affairs.

Williams, Raymond. 1976. *Marxism and Literature.* Oxford: Oxford University Press.

3

Capitalizing (on) Gifting

Mark C. Taylor

WELL, HERE WE ARE AGAIN—gathered together to talk to each other like so many times before. We do, of course, all know each other, even if we have not met previously. It is, after all, a small, rather exclusive club that nonmembers either ignore or insist is useless. We do not necessarily disagree with the assessment of others; to the contrary, we seem to value our uselessness.

Not only are we all more or less familiar to each other, but we are gathering once again to discuss among ourselves the all-too-familiar question of the gift and perhaps sacrifice. We are meeting, that is to say, to consider among ourselves precisely that which is useless. This conversation has been going on for at least thirty years, ever since we first started hearing about restricted and general economies. Though that might have been the beginning for many of us, it was, of course, only the latest chapter in a much longer story, which can be traced through Derrida, Marion, Levinas, Lévi-Strauss, Bataille, Lacan, Mauss, and Durkheim back to that unavoidable point of origin: Hegel. We know what's about to occur because we've all been here before.

And that's why I must begin with a confession, a true confession: I didn't want to come to this conference; I really did not want to come. What's the point of yet another conference on "The Gift and Sacrifice"? We've all been there, done that. What can there possibly be left to say? I, for one, have nothing to add—absolutely nothing. And yet I am here. Why? Why did I agree to sacrifice time I don't have to come to a conference I don't want to attend? One reason is, of course, to see friends: to enjoy your presence and our conversation. But such pleasure would not have been sufficient to bring me to Houston, were it not for something else. I have come because I am hopelessly indebted to Edith. I have no illusion about the possibility of my presence repaying that debt. But when she called, I knew I could not refuse. It's all that responsibility stuff that she was the first to show us that Levinas had taught us.

Having accepted her invitation, however, I incurred further obligations. First, I would have to offer something to you, and second, I would have to play by the rules of our little game of give-and-take. What could I possibly offer, when, as I have already confessed, I have *nothing* to add? The rules of our game dictate that I begin with a title. Thus, I offer you "Capitalizing (on) Gifting." My remarks will be rather speculative. As always, such speculation is based on a wager: I am betting that the sacred, the work of art, and money or, perhaps, capital are inseparable. My interest, however, is not merely in religion, art, and economics, as if this were not enough; I am also interested in our interest in the gift. Why are we so obsessed with it? Why are we so interested in the gift at this precise moment of our history? Does our preoccupation have anything to do with the crisis of the business that employs all of us?

Before I begin (because I am, after all, still trying to figure out how to begin), I would like to offer a word of clarification about the practice of gifting. Gifting, as we know all too well by now, is supposed to be an expenditure without return. Some of the complexities of gifting can be discovered in an unlikely place: the United States tax code. Our current legal statutes make it clear that there are different kinds of gifts with different implications for taxation. In some cases these so-called gifts have a significant return in the form of the deferral of taxation; in others, the return for the donor is less evident. It is important to note that gifts are treated differently for income-tax and gift/estate tax purposes. As legal expert Clifford Ruprecht points out, the same payment can be a gift for the purposes of the gift tax, but not for the purposes of the income tax. The gift might be taxable to the donor under the gift tax and also to the donee as income tax.

We all remember the infamous example of Mark McGwire's sixty-second home-run ball during the 1998 baseball season. When some people said they would give the ball to McGwire without any payment in return, tax experts raised the possibility that the donor as well as McGwire would be liable to taxation. Public outrage forced the Internal Revenue Service to declare an exception in this case. The gift tax uses an "objective" definition and the income tax a "subjective" definition. For gift-tax purposes, that is, to determine whether the donor is liable for tax on the transfer, the inquiry is completely market oriented: a gift is a completed, irrevocable transfer for "less than full and adequate consideration in money or money's worth." Give someone something, and get less than its equivalent value in return and you have made a gift for tax purposes. Donative intent is not required, and the subjective states of the donor and recipient are irrelevant. For the donor, the return is not in money received but in money not paid in the form of taxation. For income purposes, donative intent is the key to the law. A gift is a transfer stemming from (and I am now quoting from case law) "a detached and disinterested generosity" and must not be business related. Here, as in the previous example, for the donor the return is not in money received but in money not paid in the form of taxes. Paradoxically, the only way to keep your money is to give it away.

A final example from inheritance law complicates matters even further. As some of you probably know and others will eventually discover, gifting is a legal strategy devised to help one's heirs avoid paying inheritance taxes. One can currently gift heirs a lifetime total of 650,000 dollars without either the donor or the recipient incurring tax liability. The catch is that this gift must be irrevocable: it must, in other words, be made with no expectation of return. Moreover, such a gift is of no monetary benefit to the donor during his or her lifetime. The benefit, which is enjoyed by one's heirs, is the avoidance of inheritance tax on the gifted assets. In all of these cases, the gift remains entangled in economic exchanges that make some kind of return unavoidable. It is, in other words, impossible not to capitalize (on) gifting. I trust—trust and trusts complicate all of this even further—that I need not add that the activity in which we are engaged depends directly on the intricate laws of gifting. Educational institutions as we know them would not exist without the gift-tax law. We are capitalizing on gifting here and now. Perhaps this is part of the unspoken reason for our interest in the gift. I am betting that there will be a return on my investment in this preliminary discurus at the end of my speculation.

With these thoughts in mind, let us return to what is for most of us more familiar terrain. The locus classicus for much of the recent discussion of the problem of the gift is, of course, Derrida's essay on Bataille entitled "From Restricted to General Economy: A Hegelianism without Reserve." For reasons that I will attempt to make clear in what follows, Derrida, following Bataille, sees in Hegelianism a transparent translation of the foundational principles of a capitalistic market economy. Conversely, capitalism, from this perspective, can be understood as the outworking or incarnation of Hegelian Spirit. Looking back on Derrida's text three decades after its initial publication, it is obvious that the rudiments of the interpretation of the gift presented in a work like *The Gift of Death* are already present in his reading of Bataille. While the notion of the gift was central in French sociology from the time of Mauss's seminal essay, what interests Derrida is Lévi-Strauss's distinctive appropriation of Mauss's argument to develop his interpretation of kinship structures. For Lévi-Strauss, women function as tokens of exchange or currency whose circulation establishes social hierarchies and patterns. From this point of view, the economy of social relations is maintained by regulating the flow of women. Derrida's analysis of Lévi-Strauss's argument hinges on his characteristic gesture of turning the text against itself to expose what it says by not saying it. In this case, Derrida develops an "aneconomic" reading of the gift. If a gift is encompassable within an economic system, it is not a gift in the strict sense of the term. To give a gift with the expectation of return is not to give a "real" gift: such gifting is just a form of self-interest. If gifting were possible, it would have to fall "outside" every exchange relationship. A "real" rather than a pseudo-gift would pull the foundation out from under structuralism, and much else.

In order to develop his argument, Derrida turns to Hegel by way of Bataille. This move from structuralism to Hegelianism reflects the tendency of French philosophers, artists, and critics to read Hegelianism as proto-structuralism and structuralism as latter-day Hegelianism. The issue for Derrida, as well as Bataille, involves alternative readings of negation or negativity. Though no thinker in the history of philosophy had thought the negative more thoroughly than Hegel, Bataille insists that he still had not thought negativity radically enough. In one of the most memorable passages in the *Phenomenology,* Hegel writes:

> But the life of spirit is not the life that shrinks from death and keeps itself untouched by devastation, but rather the life that endures it and maintains itself in it. It wins its truth only when, in utter dismemberment, it finds itself. . . . Spirit is this power only by looking the negative in the face, and tarrying with it. This tarrying with the negative is the magical power that converts it into being (1977, 19).

Having recognized "the power of the negative" in nature and history, Hegel proceeds to double and thereby simultaneously negate and preserve negation. Or so he claims. Double negation is the logical structure of the Hegelian idea and, as such, forms the foundation of the entire system. The "magical" negation of negation is the *recuperative* gesture through which every loss turns into a gain. This is, of course, a philosophical rendering of the economy of salvation: resurrection always follows crucifixion; loss is never final, because the return on every investment is guaranteed by the One upon whom we can always bank.

Neither Bataille nor Derrida is convinced that the signature Hegelian operation of double negation actually preserves the negative. If Spirit finds itself in and through its own negation, then the only thing that is truly lost through the long and admittedly tortuous dialectical process is negation. Investment in the labor of history is prudent, because every loss turns into profit. What Hegel cannot bear is unredeemable expenditure. Since Hegel believes that loss is impossible and return is inevitable, Bataille labels the Hegelian economy "restricted." Derrida explains Bataille's point:

> The phenomenology of spirit (and phenomenology in general) corresponds to a restricted economy: restricted to commercial values . . . a "science dealing with the utilization of wealth," limited to the meaning and the established value of objects, and to their *circulation.* The *circularity* of absolute knowledge could dominate, could comprehend only this circulation, only the *circuit of reproductive consumption.* The absolute production and destruction of value, the exceeding energy as such, the energy which "can only be lost without the slightest aim, consequently without any meaning"—all this escapes phenomenology as restricted economy (Derrida 1978, 271).

So understood, the Hegelian economy works by securing a return on every investment. This is what makes the system so interesting. The Hegelian economy is restricted to and by the principle
of principle and interest and the law of return, which lends, as it
were, the circulation of both speculative currency and speculative
philosophy their currency. The general economy, by contrast,
designates that which exceeds or falls "outside" the restricted
economy. Writing in *The Accursed Share*, Bataille defines the general economy:

> Changing from perspectives of restrictive economy to those of gen-
> eral economy actually accomplishes a Copernican transformation:
> a reversal of thinking—and of ethics. If part of wealth . . . is
> doomed to destruction or at least to unproductive use without any
> possible profit, it is logical, even inescapable, to surrender commodi-
> ties without return. . . . Woe to those who, to the very end, insist on
> regulating the movement that exceeds them with the narrow mind
> of the mechanic who changes a tire (Bataille 1991, 26–27).

The machinations of the restricted economy, it seems, end with
Hegel spinning his wheels on tires that are flat. Instead of always
seeking to turn a profit by turning every loss into a gain and every
negative into a positive, the general economy exposes an unlawful
prodigality in which expenditure remains unproductive. It is important to note that for Bataille every economy is, in some sense,
a consumer economy. The distinction between the restricted and
the general economy does not turn on the question of consumption but on the issue of utility. While the restricted economy always involves useful consumption, the general economy, in
Bataille's words, is dedicated "to that glorious operation, to useless consumption" (1991, 23). The difference between the restricted and the general economy is, therefore, the distinction
between useful and useless consumption. While the former is consumption that works by turning expenditure into profit, useless
expenditure is without return and, hence, is unproductive and,
by extension, purposeless.

Bataille associates the endless or purposeless prodigality of useless consumption with both the sacred and art. As opposed to the
sacred, the profane always involves work, which presupposes the
ceaseless deferral of the end for which one strives. Bataille elabo-

rates his understanding of work by describing the instrumentality of the means-end relationship entailed in utilitarianism of the tool:

> The tool has no value in itself—like the subject, or the world, or the elements that are of the same nature as the subject or the world—but only in relation to an anticipated result. The time spent making it directly establishes its utility, its subordination of the one who uses it with the end in view, and its subordination to this end; at the same time it establishes the clear distinction between the end and means and it does so in the very terms that its appearance has defined (Bataille 1989, 28).

Through a paradoxical double reversal, the deferral of the end retrospectively constitutes the inaccessibility of the beginning (that is, the past), and the originary loss of the beginning prospectively constitutes the endless approach of the end (the future). The duplicity of this repression constitutes time and history by ceaselessly displacing the present as such. The sacred, by contrast, restores the lost intimacy of presence by sacrificing everything that is useful. Bataille's account of the festival indirectly recalls Durkheim's analysis of rituals in terms of "effervescence":

> The sacred is that prodigious effervescence of life that, for the sake of duration, the order of things holds in check, and that this holding changes into a breaking loose, that is, into violence. It constantly threatens to break the dikes, to confront productive activity with the precipitate and contagious movement of a purely glorious consumption. The sacred is exactly comparable to the flame that destroys the wood by consuming it (Bataille 1989, 52–53).

Rejecting Freud's economic reading of the festival as a quasi-cybernetic mechanism of self-regulation through psycho-social tension reduction, Bataille insists that this consumption has no end beyond itself and, thus, is its own end. The sacred, like being itself, is *ohne warum*.

When framed in these terms, Bataille's argument becomes considerably more familiar. His distinction between a restricted and general economy in terms of the useful and the useless, or the purposeful and the purposeless, can be traced to Kant's third *Critique* and, of course, beyond. Kant explains the difference between purposiveness and purposiveness without purpose by comparing the mechanism to the organism. While in a machine, means and end are externally related, in an organism, means and end are internally related. The principle of "intrinsic finality" stipulates that "an organized natural product is one in which every part is reciprocally both ends and means." According to Kant:

> The parts of a thing combine of themselves into the unity of a whole by being reciprocally cause and effect of their form. For this is the only way in which it is possible that the idea of the whole may conversely, or reciprocally, determine in its turn the form and combination of all the parts, not as cause . . . but as the epistemological basis upon which the systematic unity of the form and combination of all the manifold contained in the given matter becomes cognizable to the person estimating it (1973, 24, 21).

Since means and end are reciprocally related, the parts of the organism do not point beyond themselves to an external telos but constitute their own end or purpose. The notion of inner teleology defines the structure not only of natural organisms but also of the beautiful work of art. In developing his analysis of aesthetic judgment, Kant consistently defines the work of art by contrasting it with every form of utility. Art—or, more precisely, fine art—is nonutilitarian and hence useless. The purpose of *l'oeuvre d'art,* in other words, is nothing other than itself. For this reason, aesthetic judgment must be disinterested. Interest—be it psychological or economic—points beyond itself to something else or something other than itself and, therefore, is not purposeless or useless. If read in this way, Kant's account of purposiveness without purpose can be understood as an anticipation Bataille's general economy. The work of art falls outside the unavoidable utilitarianism of every restricted economy.

It is impossible to overestimate the importance of Kant's analysis of the work of art for subsequent philosophical reflection and artistic practice. By recasting the classical account of final causality, Kant redefines the terms in which art, philosophy, and religion are interpreted. As Schleiermacher's *Speeches on Religion* amply demonstrate, religion is reconceived in terms of art at the precise moment that art displaces the traditional role of religion. More important than Schliermacher's aesthetic religiosity, however, is Hegel's religio-aesthetic philosophy. The Hegelian system is, in effect, a logical articulation and outworking of Kant's pivotal notion of purposiveness without purpose. Hegel explicates the logical structure of reciprocity of means and end in inner teleology in terms of self-referentiality or self-reflexivity. As we shall see in what follows, Hegel's analysis of the structure of self-reflexivity leads directly to Marx's interpretation of capital and indirectly to the understanding of the self-referentiality of the work of art that underlies so much twentieth-century aesthetic theory and artistic practice.

Before proceeding to a more detailed consideration of the complex interplay of art, religion, and economics by way of Hegel, Marx, and twentieth-century art, I want to pause to ask why the notion of the uselessness or purposelessness of the work of art emerged at precisely the time it did. The answer to this question might suggest why our preoccupation with the notion of the gift has emerged in recent years.

As I have suggested, the movement from the eighteenth to the nineteenth century can be understood in terms of a shift from mechanistic to organic concepts and metaphors for interpreting the world and human experience. Far from an idle philosophical and artistic idea, the notion of the organism reflected social analyses and criticisms that were widespread among many leading artists and writers during the closing decade of the eighteenth century. While poets and philosophers used the trope of the machine to describe the personal and social fragmentation wrought by the spread of a market economy and industrial capitalism, they invoked the organism to figure unified society, which existed in the past and should be realized again in the future.

In a world governed by the competitive laws of an industrial economy, class divisions emerge, which create conflict among and within individuals. In *Letters on the Aesthetic Education of Man,* Schiller is keenly aware of the toll that modern industrialism takes on workers. For him, workers in this situation are condemned to play the role of the fragment alienated from the whole. As Schiller indicates by the title of his work, the artist will lead people from the fallen condition of fragmentation to the kingdom of organic community in which wholeness is restored. The realization of this integrated socio-political totality would be the concrete actualization of Kant's work of art, which is, quite obviously, an aesthetic rendering of the kingdom of God on earth. Schiller implies that there is actually a purpose in purposelessness and, by extension, an interest in disinterestedness. What interests, then, are served by purposelessness?

With the decline of aristocratic and ecclesiastical power and the emergence of the bourgeoisie wrought by the advent of modern industrialism, the conditions of artistic production and consumption changed significantly. When the medieval patronage system collapsed, art was transformed into a commodity, and artists had to compete in the marketplace. Art no longer was produced exclusively for wealthy patrons who enjoyed leisure and were unburdened by the necessity to work; it now had to be marketed by effectively addressing consumers with different interests. The emergence of a market economy created a new class between workers (or producers) and the aristocracy (nonproducers). The members of this new class sought to identify themselves by cultural markers of social difference. The interests of the artist and the consumer intersected in a search for cultural artifacts that were not completely subject to market forces. The creation and possession of works of art came to serve as a means of establishing social distinction. For art to serve this function, however, it had to be clearly distinguished from all commodities and could not have any utilitarian end. Art, in the strict sense of the term, became high or pure art, which was different from crafts, mass art, and popular art. "By an apparent paradox," Bourdieu points out, "as the art market began to develop, writers and artists found themselves able to affirm the irreducibility of the work of art to the status of a simple article of merchandise and, at the same time, the singularity of the intellectual and artistic condition" (1985, 16). This distinction between high and low art formulated at the end of the eighteenth century remains decisive throughout the twentieth century.

In an essay that exercised enormous influence for both art criticism and artistic practice, "The Avant-Garde and Kitsch," Clement Greenberg writes:

> Kitsch is a product of the industrial revolution, which urbanized the masses of Western Europe and America and established what is called universal literacy. . . . To fill the demand for the new market,

a new commodity was devised: ersatz culture, kitsch, destined for those who, insensible to the values of genuine culture, are hungry nevertheless for the diversion that only culture of some sort can provide. Kitsch . . . welcomes and cultivates this insensibility. It is the source of its profits. Kitsch is mechanical and operates by formulas. Kitsch is vicarious experience and faked sensations. . . . Kitsch is the epitome of all that is spurious in the life of our times. Kitsch pretends to demand nothing of its customers except their money—not even their time (1988, 11–12).

In contrast to mechanically produced and economically motivated kitsch, true art demands time, which nonworkers apparently have, and surplus money, which they apparently do not need. Redrawing the circle that joins art, religion, and economics, Greenberg concludes: "The avant-garde poet or artist tries in effect to imitate God by creating something valid solely in its own terms" (1988, 9). The precious work of art is a sacred object that can only be properly enjoyed in disinterested contemplation.

Ever sensitive to the subtle circulation of cultural capital, Bourdieu distinguishes a restricted economy—through which so-called high art circulates—from large-scale cultural production, which is at work in mass or popular art. It is important to note that Bourdieu's restricted production is the opposite of Bataille's restricted economy. In "The Market of Symbolic Goods," Bourdieu writes:

The system of production and circulation of symbolic goods is defined as the system of objective relations among different institutions, functionally defined by their role in the division of labor of production, reproduction, and diffusion of symbolic goods. The field of production per se owes its own structure to the opposition between the field of restricted production as a system of producing cultural goods objectively destined for a public of producers of cultural goods, and the field of large-scale cultural production, specifically organized with a view to the production of cultural goods destined for non-producers of cultural goods, "the public at large" (Bourdieu 1985, 17).

In restricted production, artists—and, for reasons that soon will become apparent, intellectuals—produce for other artists rather than for nonartists or the masses. Only those who create art can truly understand it. This self-understanding of creative artists is a specific reaction to the loss of patronage and the corresponding necessity for artists to confront the realities of the marketplace. Replacing one master with another, liberation from the patron leads to servitude to the market.

It follows that those "inventions" of Romanticism—the representation of culture as a kind of superior reality, irreducible to the vulgar demands of economics and the ideology of free, disinterested "creation" founded on the spontaneity of innate inspiration—appear to be just so many reactions to the pressures of an anonymous market. It is significant that the appearance of an anonymous "bourgeois" public and the irruption of methods borrowed from the economic order coincide with the rejection of bourgeois aesthetics and with the methodical attempt to distinguish the artist and the intellectual from other commoners by positing the unique products of "creative genius" against interchangeable products, utterly and completely reducible to their commodity value. Concomitantly, the absolute autonomy of the "creator" is affirmed, as is his claim to recognize as recipient of his art none but an alter ego, another creator—whose understanding of works of art presupposes an identical creative disposition (Bourdieu 1985, 16–17).

True artists, in other words, talk only to themselves and do not deign to lower themselves to address the masses or a popular audience. Their conversation is, of course, idle chatter because it has no discernible practical relevance. Far from productive work, art, it seems, is frivolous play.

It is painfully obvious that this desire to escape market forces is as idle as the chatter that promotes art with no purpose other than itself. Though artists and intellectuals are often inclined to deny it, they need the very market that they abhor. At the end of the eighteenth century, this need was met by members of the emerging bourgeoisie who, as I have noted, were looking for a way to establish their difference from peasants and workers. By consuming art that was inaccessible to the masses, the new governing class found a cultural marker that secured their social distinction. But since these new consumers were not themselves cultural producers, they had to undergo an aesthetic education. This made them privy to the secrets of creative genius and the lessons of priceless art. While Bourdieu illustrates this point with the example of literature, his insight applies to all of the liberal arts.

To appreciate the gulf separating experimental art, which originates in the field's own internal dialectic, from popular art forms, one might consider the evolutionary logic of literary language use. As this restricted language is produced in accordance with social relations whose dominant feature is the quest for distinction, its use obeys what one might term "the gratuitousness principle." Its manipulation demands the almost reflexive knowledge of schemes of expression, which are transmitted by an education explicitly aimed at inculcating the allegedly appropriate categories (Bourdieu 1985, 22).

Such education cannot be practical but has to be resolutely impractical. The value of this education, like art itself, is a distinctive uselessness. As we have come to suspect, however, it is precisely this uselessness that proves to be so useful. The more restricted the club, the more valuable membership in it becomes. Value, like desire, is created by restriction. The principles of Bourdieu's restricted production undergo a dialectical reversal, to form something approximating Bataille's restricted economy. As we shall see, when Bataille's argument is pushed to its conclusion, it also suffers a dialectical reversal, which reveals the inescapability of capitalizing (on) gifting.

The undeniable usefulness of uselessness and unavoidable interest at work in disinterest underscore the recuperative capacity of market forces. Ever expanding in ways that cannot be predicted, the market strengthens itself by repeatedly incorporating what is designed to resist it, and thereby effectively turns resistance to its own ends. In a certain sense, this process of recuperation, appropriation, and incorporation seems to enact something like the Hegelian dialectic of double negation. To see how this might be so, let us return to Marx's appropriation of Hegel.

As is well known, Hegel maintains that speculative philosophy brings artistic and religious images and representations to conceptual clarity. From the perspective of speculative philosophy, Kant's account of inner teleology at work in the beautiful work of art is isomorphic with the self-reflexive structure of the Trinitarian God. Philosophically comprehended, the Christian doctrine of God reveals the logical structure of the Hegelian Absolute. As the self-reflexive principle, which is the ground of being, the Absolute is the universal medium in and through which identities and differences are created and sustained. By moving beyond the Aristotelian principle of noncontradiction, it becomes possible to discern the syllogistic structure of the Hegelian Absolute.

I—U—P
[individuality—universality—particularity]

The middle term of this syllogism is indeed the unity of the extremes, but a unity in which abstraction is made from their determinateness; it is the indeterminate universal. But since this universal is at the same time distinguished as abstract from the extremes as determinate, it is itself still a determinate relative to them, and the whole is a syllogism whose relation to its Concept has now to be considered. The middle term, as the universal, is the subsuming term or predicate to both its extremes, and does not occur as subsumed or as subject. Insofar, therefore, as it is supposed to correspond, as species of syllogism, to the syllogism, it can do so only on the condition that when one relation I—U already possesses the proper relationship, the other relation U—P also possesses it (Hegel 1969, 678).

The species of the syllogism is the currency that forms the medium for every type of exchange. Since the species of the syllogism is the rational articulation of the Eucharistic species, there seems to be if not an identity at least a very close relationship between God or the Absolute on the one hand and, on the other, currency or money. This relationship, which remains implicit in Hegel's argument, becomes explicit in Marx's analysis of money.

"Money," Marx declares, "is the god among commodities" (1973, 22). This god is simultaneously immanent in and transcendent to worldly processes, which appear to be thoroughly secular. Marx clarifies his cryptic identification of God and money when he writes: "Money is the incarnation of exchange value" (1973, 163). Since capital is "the most developed form of money," God eventually appears as capital, and capital is ultimately revealed to be divine. According to conventional wisdom, Marx develops his dialectical materialism by turning Hegel on his head and reinterpreting speculative logic in terms of concrete processes of production. While this reading of Marx is not incorrect, it tends to obscure the extent of his debt to Hegel. Since Marx formulates his analysis of capital by appropriating Hegel's interpretation of Spirit, capital functions in Marxist economics like God, Spirit, and the Absolute function in Hegelian philosophy. Hegel's Absolute is, in Aristotle's terms, the universal equivalent, which establishes the identity of differences. Marx, in effect, translates this speculative idea into economic terms. Money, he argues, is the mediating third, which, as the "metamorphosed shape of all commodities," secures the unity of differences and thereby makes the system exchange possible. He expresses the structural relation between money and commodities with this formula:

$$C—M—C$$
[commodity—money—commodity]

This equation summarizes the two moments of exchange: sale, in which commodity is transformed into money (C—M); and purchase, in which money is transformed into commodity (M—C). The currency of exchange allows opposites to flow into each other.

In light of the foregoing remarks about the structure of the speculative idea, there should be little doubt that Marx actually appropriates Hegel's speculative logic to formulate the logic of money and, by extension, of capital. The logic of capital conforms to the syllogistic structure of Hegel's Absolute Idea. Just as universal Spirit unites individuality and particularity (I—U—P), so the universal machinations of money and capital mediate particular commodities (C—M—C). Marx invokes religious terms to describe money: "If money appears as the general commodity in all places, so also does it in all times. It maintains itself as wealth at all times. Its specific durability. It is the treasure which neither rusts nor moths eat up. All commodities are only transitory money; money is the permanent commodity. Money is the omnipresent commodity" (Marx 1973, 231).

Far from static, the permanence of money is its ceaseless circulation. As money assumes its final form in capital, the self-reflexivity of the exchange process becomes explicit. When exchange value no longer is anchored in use value, "growing wealthy is an end in itself" (Marx 1973, 270). Exchange value posits itself as such only by realizing itself, that is, by increasing its value. Money (as returned to itself from circulation) as capital has lost its rigidity, and from a tangible thing has become a process (1973, 263).

Marx's argument again turns on his reading of Hegel. In Hegel's speculative logic, everything becomes itself in and through its own other; just as the Father, who in himself is also the Son, and the Son, who in himself is also the Father, are united through Spirit, so every particular entity includes its other within itself as a condition of its own actuality. This structure of identity-in-difference and difference-in-identity is "the universal process" through which everything arises and passes away. Expressed in terms of the speculative syllogism, the universal is the particular and the particular is the universal. Marx translates Hegel's speculative universal into the universal equivalent and interprets specific commodities as particularities, which are essentially concrete universals.

The transition from simple exchange value and its circulation to capital can also be expressed in this way: within circulation, exchange value appears double—once as commodity, again as money. If it is in one aspect, it is not in the other. This holds for every particular commodity. But the wholeness of circulation, regarded in itself, lies in the fact that the same exchange value, exchange value as subject, posits itself once as commodity, another time as money, and that it is just this movement of positing itself in this dual character and of preserving itself in each of them as its opposite, in the commodity as money and in money as commodity. This in itself is present in simple circulation, but is not posited in it. Exchange value posited as the unity of commodity and money is capital, and this positing itself appears as the circulation of capital (Marx 1973, 266.)

Since the commodity is both itself and a concrete instantiation of capital, capital, which posits itself as other in the commodity, relates itself to itself in and through its own other. The self-referentiality of capital is a further extension of the self-reflexivity of the Absolute Idea.

Capital closes the circle of money's self-becoming. Within a capitalist economy, investment is always calculated to yield the most profitable return. In this autotelic process, the purpose of the economy is nothing other than its self-perpetuation.

In the circulation of capital, the point of departure is posited as the terminal point and the terminal point is posited as the point of departure. The capitalist himself is the point of departure and of return. He exchanges money for the conditions of production, produces, realizes the product (that is, transforms it into money), and then begins the process anew. The circulation of money, regarded for itself, necessarily becomes extinguished in money as a static thing. The circulation of capital constantly ignites itself anew, divides into its different moments, and is a *perpetuum mobile* (Marx 1973, 516).

The economy, like speculative philosophy, "exhibits itself as a *circle* returning upon itself, the end being wound back into the beginning, the simple ground, by the mediation; this circle is moreover a *circle of circles*, for each individual member is ensouled by the method is reflected into itself, so that in returning into the beginning it is at the same time the beginning of a new member" (Hegel 1969, 842). Perpetually in motion, the circle of circles is the divine pulse of an economy that knows no bounds.

Marx's analysis of capitalism represents an unintentionally ironic reversal of the idea that began in Kant's investigation of the beautiful work of art. As we have seen, Kant attempts to escape the utilitarian mechanisms of the market by articulating the structure of the beautiful work of art in which means and ends are reciprocally related in such a way that artistic value is inherent in the work itself. From the point of view of the market, such intrinsic value is useless. Post-Kantian poets and philosophers, the most important of whom is Hegel, extend Kant's interpretation of art to an all-encompassing epistemological and ontological principle. When logically formulated, the self-reflexivity of the Hegelian idea appears to embody a structure of double negation that turns every loss into profit. Marx, in turn, capitalizes on Hegel's speculation by rendering capitalism speculative. With this unexpected twist, the aesthetic idea that had been designed to escape market forces becomes the grounding structure of the market itself.

This, as Derrida argues, is Bataille's point when he insists that Hegelian philosophy is a restricted economy. And this is the economy that both Bataille and Derrida struggle to escape, through the strange logic or alogic of the gift. As an expenditure without return, the gift is supposed to be economically useless. The cultural manifestations of the gratuitousness of gifting are art, more specifically literature, and religion. But is the uselessness of Bataille's and Derrida's gift any more successful in escaping economic restrictions than Kant's beautiful work of art or Hegel's aesthetic-religious-philosophical idea? Do Bataille and Derrida finally affirm what they struggle to deny by capitalizing (on) gifting?

In an effort to answer these difficult questions, let us return to Marx's account of money. Money, we have seen, is the universal equivalent that makes the exchange of commodities possible. As the condition of the possibility of exchange, money itself cannot be exchanged. If money were to become a commodity that is exchanged for other commodities, then another general equivalent would be needed to facilitate the exchange process. Apart from something like a first cause or unmoved mover, the series of substitutions is endless and, thus, the exchange process can never get going.

This point can be made in different terms: the exchange of commodities presupposes a certain surplus or excess, which is neither precisely inside nor outside the economic system. The distinguishing trait of this excess is its uselessness. If the surplus is useful it meets needs and, therefore, is transformed into a commodity that can be exchanged for other commodities. Though its forms are many—gold, silver, copper, paper, bits, light—the name of this useless excess is money. Describing the transition from barter to a money economy, Marx writes:

> Commodities, first of all, enter into the process of exchange just as they are. The process then differentiates them into commodities and money, and thus produces an external opposition corresponding to the internal opposition inherent in them, as being at once use-values and values. Commodities as use-values now stand opposed to money as exchange-value. On the other hand, opposing sides are commodities, unities of use-value and value. But this unity of differences manifests itself at two opposite poles, at each pole in an opposite way. Being poles, they are as necessarily opposite as they are connected. On the one side of the equation we have an ordinary commodity, which is in reality a use-value. Its value is expressed only ideally in its price, by which it is equated to its opponent, the gold, as the real embodiment of its value. On the other hand the gold, in its metallic reality, ranks as the embodiment of value, as money. Gold, as gold, is exchange-value itself (1967, 104).

Gold as gold—the intrinsic value of gold is the condition of the possibility of the system of exchange. What makes exchange possible cannot be exchanged but must be held in reserve. This restriction on circulation is inseparably bound to circulation, because it is what makes the flow of commodities possible. In this way, gold or its equivalent is the excess that lubricates the wheels of the economy. If there were excessive expenditures without adequate reserves—reserves kept securely in crypts or vaults—the system of exchange, it seems, would collapse.

But gold reserves have disappeared and the economy has not faltered. To the contrary, the expenditure of gold reserves has fueled the fires of consumer capitalism. This point is not merely speculative but is also historical. In the fall of 1971, the United States sent shock waves through the world economy by decoupling the dollar from gold. Since the value of other currencies were at the time linked to the dollar, this decision had serious repercussions for all countries. After futile efforts to maintain fixed exchange rates for one year, currencies were left to float freely in a market that was increasingly deregulated. Far from the collapse of the economic system, the sacrifice of the gold standard created the conditions for the spread of global capitalism. Gold, it seems, is the gift that keeps on giving. The real gift that fuels this economy, however, is not gold as such but unrestricted spending. Released from every transcendental referent, consumer capitalism is free to stage a virtual potlatch, which is energized by excessive consumption.

Having recognized the way in which the uselessness of the work of art and self-reflexivity of the philosophical idea actually reflect and promote the utilitarian markets they are supposed to escape or subvert, Bataille, and Derrida following him, attempt to identify a more radical exteriority that cannot be reappropriated in what they label a restricted economy. The gratuitous expenditure of gifting, they argue, exceeds the bounds of every restricted economy. But the general economy that gifting is supposed to generate is, in the final analysis, indistinguishable from consumer capitalism. Just as the purposelessness of Kant's work of art and Hegel's Idea are embodied in the machinations of speculative capitalism, so the excess of Bataille's and Derrida's gift operates in capital and the gratuitous consumption it promotes. Through a reversal that seems to be speculative, Bataille and Derrida affirm what they claim to deny. Once again, the recuperative powers of market capitalism seem to be irresistible.

We are, of course, every bit as guilty as Bataille and Derrida. Indeed, our guilt is inseparable from our debt to them. As we all know by now, Schuld is Schuld. On one level, our guilt is a symptom of our endless efforts to capitalize on the gift of their texts by attempting to turn them to our own profit. But the issue is more complex than this rather straightforward debt structure suggests. By capitalizing on the gift we have received from others and passing it on to those who come after us, we become ever more deeply entangled in the economy of guilt and redemption.

In closing, I would like to return to three questions I posed at the beginning of my speculative reflections: Why are we so obsessed with the gift? Why are we so interested in the gift at this precise moment of our history? Does our preoccupation have anything to do with the crisis of the business that employs all of us?

Our activity here and now, I have suggested, depends on complex practices of gifting regulated by the governmental codes of the Internal Revenue Service. We depend on the generosity of others. As academics and intellectuals, we often try vainly to protect ourselves from pollution by filthy lucre. Moreover, many of us tend to be highly critical of the corrupting forces of the market. And yet, we are parasites who live off the market economy. When we stop to reflect on our situation, we discover that we are caught in a double bind: we cannot do without that which we nonetheless cannot bear. The free enterprise in which we are all so heavily invested is both inside and outside the market system.

We all are painfully aware that the academic enterprise and the economy that supports it are currently under severe strain. Here, as elsewhere, the condition at the end of the twentieth century is reminiscent of the situation at the end of the eighteenth century. As we have seen, the correlative notions of fine art and high culture emerged during the closing decades of the eighteenth century in reaction to the spread of industrialism and the market economy. The supposedly disinterested work of art actually served the interests of both producers (artists and intellectuals) and consumers (the developing bourgeoisie) by providing cultural markers that were supposed to bestow social distinction.

It was precisely this uselessness that made the work of art so useful to people who were eager to claim a certain independence from market forces. Since value and intellectual accessibility were inversely proportional—that is to say, the less accessible, the more valuable and vice versa—the fine-art industry spins off an education industry dedicated to the advancement of learning, which, when carefully calculated, amounts to useless knowledge. In education as in art, the restricted and the general economy become hopelessly confused. The more restricted the economy, the more useless its products, and through a reversal that is not exactly dialectical, the more useless the product, the more useful it is as a sign of social difference.

When we shift from an industrial to a postindustrial economy, this pattern repeats itself. In an information economy, knowledge itself becomes a valuable commodity that is traded in networks that are increasingly global. This commodification of knowledge has serious consequences for the academy and how it conducts its business. When workers become knowledge workers, education per se no longer functions as a decisive marker of social distinction in the way it does in an industrial society. In a postindustrial economy, knowledge becomes the currency of the realm that fuels the fires of capitalism. As the usefulness of knowledge grows, demand for education increases.

In an effort to meet this demand, the market expands by invading the sacred precincts of the university, as well as creating new technologies and institutions for reproducing and delivering the educational product. These developments obscure longstanding social, cultural, and economic distinctions. The critical issue once again is the problem of profits. In an information economy, where knowledge is a commodity and education is big business, the line separating profit from not-for-profit practices and institutions, which was never clear in the first place, is virtually erased.

These comments do not imply that the founding distinction between profit and not-for-profit simply disappears. To the contrary, as the education market steadily expands, the purported difference between profit and not-for-profit practices and institutions is vigorously reasserted by those whose self-interest it serves. If the brief history of the University of Phoenix has proved anything, it is that the drama between high and low art, which is based upon the profitability of a restricted economy, is being re-staged in the business of so-called higher education.

This struggle is obvious in the criticism and parody of the crass commercialism of for-profit education, but it also takes more sub-tle forms in widespread suspicions about emerging media and information technologies. In a futile effort to resist the expansion of market forces, academics and intellectuals frequently resist adopting new technologies for creating, reproducing, and dis-seminating knowledge. In freely embracing their growing irrele-vance, they make their own obsolescence a value that is actively affirmed. Though this resistance is sometimes expressed in terms of high-minded principle and political purpose, its motivation, more often than not, is misguided self-interest.

It is important to stress that the developments I am tracing apply equally to all subjects and disciplines. The arts, the humani-ties, and, by extension, the liberal arts are most at risk in a system that calculates value as profitable return on investments. With growing risk to their very survival, humanists face an impossible choice: either defend themselves in terms of the market by dem-onstrating the practical usefulness of the knowledge they convey, or continue to resist the market by defending the impracticality of their knowledge and education. Defiantly courting economic disaster, many humanists choose the latter alternative.

As mechanical means of production give way to electronic means of reproduction, today's academics and intellectuals tend to repeat the strategy of eighteenth-century artists. For the intel-lectual, the knowledge that truly matters is impractical rather than practical. Impracticality, we have discovered, is a function of difficulty and hence accessibility. In education, as in art, value and accessibility are inversely proportional. The late twentieth-century academic, like the late eighteenth-century artist, does not produce work for the nonintellectual masses but for other intel-lectual producers.

Accordingly, we write for each other in books and journals that only our colleagues read, and talk to each other in conferences like this one, which are attended only by those we already know. In this setting, as in all others, the purpose of our work is nothing other than the work itself. If the work is really good—if it's as good as go(l)d—its value is intrinsic and cannot be accurately determined by the market. Indeed, success in the market raises suspicions about the value of the work. According to this transvaluation of values, the academy's gift to the world is impractical or useless knowledge.

This conclusion suggests possible answers to the questions I have been pursuing throughout these remarks. We are obsessed with the gift at this precise moment in our history because it is the expression of our highest self-interest. The logic of the gift is nothing other than the logic of the system of higher education. Not just development offices but faculties have learned how to capitalize (on) gifting.

But we cannot end with this conclusion without adding a final, perhaps supplementary note. Our collective deliberations have led us to conclude that there is no gift without sacrifice. In the economy of higher education, what is sacrificed, who sacrifices, who is sacrificed? The answers seem obvious: *we* sacrifice—and what we sacrifice is financial gain in order to contribute knowledge that is invaluable. After all, none of us went into this business for money; we had higher ideals. Moreover, we all know—or believe—that we could have made much more money if we had not gone into education.

When we are honest with ourselves, however, we are forced to admit that these answers are disingenuous. Our useless knowledge is, of course, very useful to us because it gives us lifelong employment. We are among the privileged who continue to receive a return on our investment in education. So where is the sacrifice? What is sacrificed? Who is sacrificed? Protests to the contrary notwithstanding, the sacrifice is not a self-sacrifice but is a sacrifice of others. The others we sacrifice to promote our own self-interests are our students.

The price of our useless knowledge is the sacrifice of our students. While there is a return on our investment, for at least thirty years, students have been keeping us employed by preparing themselves for lifelong unemployment. This is a *désoeuvrement* they would rather avoid but, for the most part, cannot. When it comes to the question of the gift and sacrifice, it is the students who have something to teach their teachers. We have not yet learned how to avoid capitalizing (on) gifting.

BIBLIOGRAPHY

Bataille, Georges. 1991. *The Accursed Share: An Essay on General Economy*. Vol. 1, *Consumption*. Trans. Robert Hurley. New York: Zone Books.

———. 1989. *Theory of Religion*. Trans. Robert Hurley. New York: Zone Books.

Bourdieu, Pierre. 1985. "The Market of Symbolic Goods," Poietics 14: 17.

Derrida, Jacques. 1978. "From a Restricted to General Economy: A Hegelianism Without Reserve," in *Writing and Difference*. Trans. Alan Bass. Chicago: University of Chicago Press.

Greenberg, Clement. 1988. "Avant-Garde and Kitsch," in *The Collected Essays and Criticism*. Vol. 1. Ed. John O'Brian. Chicago: University of Chicago Press.

Hegel, G. W. F. 1977. *Phenomenology of Spirit*. Trans. A. V. Miller New York: Oxford University Press.

———. 1969. *Science of Logic*. Trans. A. V. Miller. New York: Oxford University Press.

Kant, Immanuel. 1973. *Critique of Judgment*. Trans. James Meredith. New York: Oxford University Press.

Marx, Karl. 1967. *Capital*. Vol. 1. Ed. Friedrich Engles. New York: International Publishers.

———. 1973. Grundrisse. Trans. Martin Nicolaus. New York: Penguin Books.

Schiller, Friedrich. 1977. *On the Aesthetic Education of Man in a Series of Letters*. Trans. Reginald Snell. New York: Frederick Unger.

2
Community, Gift, and Sacrifice

4

"Even Steven," or "No Strings Attached"

Stephen A. Tyler

THIS PAPER addresses three issues surrounding the idea of the gift. The first concerns the structure of propositions that inform the idea of giving. The second addresses the issue of psychological individualism, and the third is a critique of the ethnological concept of the gift. The paper is divided into three sections: the first deals with the topics of propositional structure and psychologizing, the second with contrastive semantic analysis, and the third with ethnographic exempla.

PART I: "WHAT GIVES?" DADADA

Propositional Structure

It is useful to remember that in English, when one says "I give this gift," it expresses the semantic structure of the verb *give*. *Give* is a three-place predicate that involves three arguments. Thus in the proposition "x gives z to y," x is the giver, z the given, and y the "given to" or recipient. English has exceptions to this structure, in which the recipient argument is deleted or suppressed, as in "I give up," "I give in," "I gave birth." Also, there are sometimes peculiar "givens," as in: "He gave her measles," "I gave him a kick." And finally, there are instances in which the giver is suppressed or, as we sometimes say, is "understood," as in such command/entreaties as "give 'em hell," "gimme a break!"

I cite these anomalies because I want to argue that they open up possibilities for understanding the complex of the gift in ways that overcome some of Derrida's (1992) objections to the possibility of the gift as a real or "true" gift. To put it differently, much of the argument about the gift hangs from the normative structure of the propositional semantics of *give* in English or other related Indo-European languages. Thus, the major issues are: (1) the intentions of the giver; (2) the nature of the gift; and (3) the obligations of the recipient.

The Intention of the Giver

Many discussions of the gift take those situations where the giver expects a return as the prototype of giving. To put it differently, all real giving is exchanging. It is as if the proposition "x gives z to y" automatically entails its reciprocal, "y gives z' to x." In other words, both x and y understand that z is not a free gift or that it has, as we say, strings attached. It is, of course, this expectation of a return that seemingly links the idea of the gift to the ideas of exchange and sacrifice. In this formulation, every act of giving, every gift, and every act of receiving a gift entails an expectation of an obligatory return of an equivalent gift. The seemingly innocuous z' in the reciprocal above is actually the basis for what can come to be the calculation of equivalent values in the determination of what kinds of things will count as the same as z. Where z = z', we have the possibility of the resolution of expectation and a cessation of exchange of z's. This is the situation we commonly call "even steven."

In Derrida's argument, any anticipation or expectation of reciprocity as a return for a gift spoils the gift. Thus it is the subject and the dative positions in the sentence that are problematic, since they already signify the idea of the subject as a complex of psychological attributes, not the least of which is that the subject is always selfish and incapable of any altruistic act. The subject's relation to the other as a giver to recipient follows the classic pattern of Hegelian subjects who enhance their own identity by overcoming the identity of the other. Behind every gift lurks the ulterior motive of the giver who expects a return, and it is the recipient's perception of the giver's ulterior motive that impels him to "give as good as he gets" in order to be free of obligation or, conversely, to be locked into an ongoing relationship of reciprocal exchanges over time. This exemplifies Bourdieu's argument in *The Logic of Practice* (1990) that the spirit of the gift always contains a more or less disguised challenge.

It is difficult to refute this dark imagery of selfishness and self-interest mitigated only by the possibility of reciprocal selfishness and self-interest, because it is intrinsic to our idea of the subject. As Derrida notes, the only possibility of a gift being a gift is that there be no subjects. Even Heidegger's antipassive formulation *es gibt,* meant to formulate something like "there is giving going on by some indefinite entity," is problematic, since it deletes recipients and gifts but still requires the subject *es.* One possibility, then, is to delete even this phony subject, and we would have something like "gives" or "giving," which may seem strange but can be understood if we assume that this is something like the middle voice in which subjects and objects are already implicated in the process of the verb *giving* without being specified or prior to it.

Subjects (givers and recipients) would not determine giving, but would instead be determined by giving. This may seem a bit odd, but it does eliminate any objections arising from the psychological characteristics of subjects. In this regard, it is worth remembering that priests officiating in the Vedic sacrifices often expressed the ritual formulae of offerings in the Sanskrit middle voice (*atmane padam,* literally "word for another"). Part of the reason for this usage was that the priest was making an offering to the gods not for himself, but for another, the *yajaman*(sacrificer). In this case, the priest did not expect a return, even though the sacrificer did expect one.

Other grammatical possibilities could likewise influence the agentive role of the subject as giver. Causatives, for example, as in "he had it given," indicate a different role for the subject such that it is not far-fetched to suppose that "he had it coming." "He had it given to him" is wonderfully ambiguous in English. Is it causative or passive? Consider also the nuanced differences of "he was given a great gift." The different roles of experiencer, experienced, and agency in these English sentences foreground or direct our attention to quite different aspects of the situation of giving.

I note these grammatical possibilities as a way of pointing out different possibilities in the roles of subjects (givers and recipients), but also as a reminder that much of what we take to be given in the discussion of the gift is, in fact, given by virtue of thinking the active voice is the prototypical case.

Datum: *The Given*

Since gifts occupy one of the object positions in the proposition (the accusative), the middle-voice situation sketched above applies as well to the gift. This grammatical move circumvents all arguments arising from the idea that some kind of sanctity or supernatural power residing in the gift impels the recipient's obligation to reciprocate. The power is in giving and is not something in the gift or something transferred from the giver to the recipient.

Psychologizing

In every instance, whether it is the giver, the given, or the recipient, arguments are infused with a kind of subjectivization in which such forces as motivation, expectation, obligation, self-interest, and self-deception are reasonable psychological attributes. It is notable, in this regard, that the gift itself is personified and given these same psychic functions, as, for example, in the arguments about Maori *hau* (Sahlins 1972). Givers, recipients, and gifts are all psychologized. This rampant psychologizing stems from the need to explain away the possibility of disinterested giving.

Disinterested giving is akin to the Kantian sublime. It is not a concept of the subject. To put it differently, psychologizing enables one to dismiss the possibility that someone might not act out of self-interest. Psychologizing makes it possible to demonstrate that what appears to be a violation of the iron law of self-interest is really just that—an appearance that masks the real self-interest at the same time as it expresses it in its most virulent form. In Bourdieu's paranoiac interpretation, this is the fiction of a disinterested exchange in which givers and receivers are simultaneously deceivers and deceived.

One way to avoid these traumas of the calculating subject is to locate the compulsion to give in a realm that transcends individual subjects. Two arguments of this type are worth noting. The first is Lévi-Strauss's structuralist argument, in which individual subjectivity is totally subsumed within the abstract relationships among groups governed by rules for establishing and maintaining the possible. The possible is only what is necessary, and in it there is no place for a calculating subject. The structure is a self-governing, timeless repetition. Structuralism, however, resolves nothing, since it merely locates the problem in a kind of dislocated transcendental ego.

A related relocation is attempted by Bourdieu. He locates the impetus that governs reciprocity not in the structure of groups but in the habitus, and in the communication of symbolic capital, which, seemingly, allows for strategic manipulation of the return of a gift. The calculating subject literally has its moment in the lapse of time between the gift and the countergift, but is actually constrained to return the gift because that's the way things are. The necessary is only what is possible.

PART II: ETHNOGRAPHIC MOMENT ONE, ON "GIVING IT AWAY"

It is gratuitous to suppose that things everywhere can be given and had on the model of the English/Indo-European words for giving. It would be interesting, for example, to look more closely at the comparative linguistics of words for giving in other languages (Newman 1999). We need not, however, go so far afield. A contrastive semantic analysis of different words for giving in English reveals important differences of subject and object involvement in giving propositions.

Consider the idea of the donor in English. It does not always make good sense to conflate the English terms *give* and *donate*, if for no other reason than that one can make a donation but cannot make a "give," which is one of the reasons we have the word *gift* in English. The difference between *give* and *donate* has to do with the idea of return. Donate, in most of its uses, does not entail an expected return from the recipient. In other words, "x gives z to y" does not imply "y gives z' to x." The donor may get something for her donation, but not from the recipient.

Organ donors are a case in point. In such cases, we are likely to say "the act of donating is its own reward," betraying our sense that the donor gets something even if it is nothing more than the sense of satisfaction for having done a good deed. Note, however, that this sense of a good deed done occurs in a kind of irrealis, a future event that cannot be part of the donor's experience. The donor cannot experience satisfaction for doing a good deed, since the deed has been done only in a kind of imaginary or virtual reality. Contracting to do a good deed and doing the deed are not the same thing. It's rather like saying, "I'm going to give someone a great gift," but without the capacity for actually doing it. In sum, the idea of organ donation must be a very marginal expression of self-interest, because the reward is too ephemeral.

The question of return raises problems about all sorts of contexts in which returns are deferred or detoured through intermediaries. Such situations defeat the idea of the donor's expectation of a return, because the sources from which a return might come are too remote or indirect for them to figure realistically in the donor's expectation of a return. In other words, the donor can neither calculate an equivalence nor realistically expect a return from unknowable sources and indeterminate times.

Then too, what of all those cases in which we give things in order to be rid of them, as, for example, donating old clothing and no-longer-useful-to-us household items to Goodwill or the Salvation Army? Do we say that the return here is just the sense of well-being that flows from having cleaned out our overburdened closets? Perhaps, but I think this stretches the notion of return beyond its elasticity. I return to this notion of gifting the unwanted in the discussion of the Indian example in Part III, but note here that we can also think of the unwanted gift from the perspectives of both giver and receiver.

Finally, these considerations about expectations draw our attention to the way this discussion proceeds exclusively at the level of the concrete, where real individuals give and receive real things within a finite period of time. There are other "give" verbs in English, such as *provide, yield,* and *afford,* that deliver a different sense of these processes and that have the added advantage of functioning at various levels of abstraction. Consider the idea of affordance in the sense of "to give or provide as a natural consequence." Gibson, for example, uses the term in this sense in his theory of perception. The natural world affords itself to our perceptions because the world and our perceptions are already linked. *Affordance* is closely akin to *yield* in the sense of *yielding grain*, a process in which the idea of intentionality is strange because there is no proper intentional or agentive subject here.

A corn plant yields grain because that is what a corn plan does. We might say it is its nature to give. True enough—people are not plants. But that does not preclude the possibility that we too might become affordances, or manifest a kind of conatus, yielding, as it were, because that is what we do. Then too, some of our acts of giving might already be affordances, if we but choose to understand them that way.

If an analysis of the contexts of meaning for different verbs in English reveals such possibilities for reinterpreting intentionality, it is even more so in the give/have verbs of other languages. This is especially the case where verbal systems have aspectual functions, such as the middle voice or other grammatical devices, that impinge on the idea of the subject's involvement in the action of the verb. Similarly we can find, as we do in English, that there is a lexicon of giving in which different "give" or "gift" words convey differently nuanced senses of giving.

In English it is already significant that we take *give* as the prototype for all kinds of giving and understand other "providing" terms as departures from this paragon—as I have done throughout this paper. While I think comparative grammar and semantics can reveal interesting possibilities, I do not undertake that task here in any systematic way, partly because such grammatical/lexical studies need to be contextualized within their co-implicated social situations.

PART III: ETHNOGRAPHIC MOMENT TWO, "INDIAN GIVERS"

The following brief account is intended as an example of the kind of contextualizing mentioned above. It concerns the discourse about the *jajmani* system in India. The example proceeds in two ways: first as an account of the traditional Hindu textual rendering of the reciprocal relations among social groups as a homology of the structure of the sacrifice. Some of this material figured in Marcel Mauss's original treatment of the gift. This is followed by a brief account of similar relationships in contemporary Indian peasant villages. It is important to note at the outset that the term *jajmani* derives from the Sanskrit root *yaj*, "to sacrifice." The textual system is illustrated in thought picture 1.

Thought picture 1 is a structural account that contains no time, or, perhaps better, refers to time as timeless relations of endless repetitions, à la Lévi-Strauss. The traditional account of social organization assumes that each social group has a distinct duty (*varna dharma*) or obligation to work. The performance of each group benefits the whole group and manifests the workings of universal order (dharma). We can understand these individual duties as expressions of a system of exchange, as the giving of the gift of one's work for the benefit of the whole, in return for which one receives the gift of the work of each of the other groups.

Exchange here is not, however, a simple manifestation of self-interest. The analysis does not start from the idea of the individual subject, but from the idea of the social whole. The intentions of individual subjects are only derivative, the result of the kind of nature attributed to them by their membership in a particular social group. Thus, for example, Brahmans give sacrifice because that is the nature of Brahmans. It is what Brahmans do because they are Brahmans. We may well object to this system, because it ranks social groups and their livelihoods in a hierarchical order that offends our sense of social equality and individual choice. It has appeared to many that this is too high a price to pay for defanging self-interest, but that is not the main point. The gravemen of the argument is that the analysis and understanding of the place of individuals in the social system need not start by assuming that the psychological principle of self-interest is the prime mover of social interaction. "You do what you do because that is who you are" speaks to self-interest only as a derivative, second-order, and even unnecessary possibility.

It must be understood that the foregoing is an account of the system as theorized and rationalized by Hindu thinkers in the *dharmasastras* (treatises on order) and has only an indirect relation to contemporary village practice. Village practice is informed by these ideas, but does not conform to them. First of all, village social units are *jatis* (typically called "castes" in Western literature) rather than *varnas,* and most villages will have many more

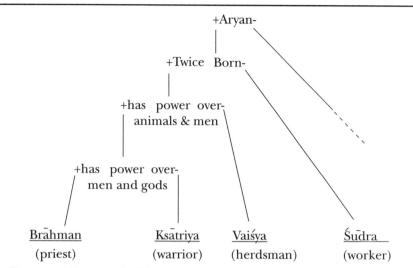

THOUGHT PICTURE I. The Hierarchical Order of the *Aryan* Community

In this representation, plus (+) indicates that a given feature is present and minus (−) that it is absent. A *Vaiśya*, for example, is defined as: + Aryan, + Twice Born, − has power over animals and men (indicating in this instance that *Vaiśya's* might have power over animals, but *not* over animals *and* men). Ranking is from right to left. Thus, a *Brāhman* ranks highest, followed in descending order by *Kṣātriyas, Vaiśyas,* and *Śūdras.* The sign + *Aryan* indicates those groups that follow *Aryan* sacrifices. Only these four groups (*varṇas*) are members of the *Aryan* community. Each *varṇa* is also defined by its social role or characteristic duty (*varṇa dharma*). Thus, *Brāhmans* perform sacrifice, *Kṣātriyas* protect the people, *Vaiśyas* provide material goods, and *Śūdras* perform service. These duties are recriprocal and reflexive, as follows: *Brāhmans* "give" sacrifice to *Brāhmans, Kṣātriyas, Vaiśyas,* and *Śūdras; Kṣātriyas* "give" protection to *Kṣātriyas, Brāhmans, Vaiśyas,* and *Śūdras; Vaiśyas* "give" material goods to *Vaiśyas, Brāhmans, Kṣātriyas,* and *Śūdras; Śūdras* "give" service to *Śūdras, Brāhmans, Kṣātriyas,* and *Vaiśyas.* These relations can be depicted as:

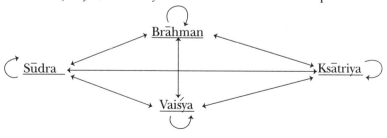

jatis than the traditional four varnas. Even so, the ideas of relativized human nature and sacrificial order are still evident in the village systems. Note that the term *jat* derives from the Sanskrit verbal root *ja,* which means "birth" and is cognate with English "genus," which gives an accurate indication of the idea of *jati.* Each jati is a separate genus and each has, as a consequence, its own essential nature that is different from the essential nature of every other jati. Human nature, in other words, is plural and relative. Instead of one universal human nature, there are multiple human natures.

We can understand the whole idea of the jajmani system in the village at the critical moment of the harvest, when the landholder's grain is cut in the fields, brought to the village threshing floor, threshed, and winnowed. The grain, formed into a large heap, is distributed by the landholder to individual representatives of all the nonlandholding jatis who have contributed to the harvest (see thought picture 2).

While thought picture 2 accurately represents the idea of reciprocity and redistribution, actual distributions are more complex. There are three different terms for the gifts that flow from landholder to participant jati, as follows:

dhanam: an offering to the gods that is a gift to the village temple and priests. It is given as the first gift.

gutha: a "contractual" share paid to craftsmen such as the carpenter and the blacksmith. They are given as the second gifts.

biksham: gift share given to all other participants. They are given last.

Landholders also give bonus shares representing different contractual situations, such as for the maintenance of a plow in irrigated fields. In addition to the dhanam given to the village priest, the potter, the washerman, and the barber receive a "priest" share called *poli cherta.* The barber and washerman are priests for the field goddess. The washerman, at seed time and harvest, brings offerings of blood and grain to the goddess of field and well. He also sprinkles some blood and grain on the threshing floor and on the borders of the fields to satisfy the demons. The barber functions as a kind of priest during the rituals surrounding

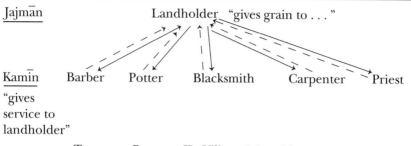

Jajmān — Landholder "gives grain to . . ."

Kamīn — Barber — Potter — Blacksmith — Carpenter — Priest
"gives
service to
landholder"

THOUGHT PICTURE II. Village *jajmāni* System.

The landholder (*jajmān*) gives grain to each of his *kamīns* (tied workers) at harvest in return for services they have performed during the year. The blacksmith and carpenter maintain the landholder's plows, the potter makes his pots, the barber cuts his hair, the priest performs rituals in the temple, and so on. At harvest each *jāti* (Barber, etc.) is entitled to take a traditional amount of grain from the grain heap on the village threshing floor. In general there is no calculation of actual services performed by recipients. Thus, x number of haircuts does not equal z number of bushels of grain. The system is based on reciprocity and redistribution.

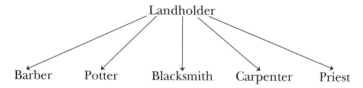

Landholder

Barber — Potter — Blacksmith — Carpenter — Priest

THOUGHT PICTURE III. The structure of *dan* ("gift")

dan is not reciprocal. The landholder gives inauspiciousness and wants no repayment from the recipient. *dan* is a non-reciprocal gift which the recipient has to take because he is less powerful than the giver.

the investiture of the sacred thread worn by high-caste men. He cuts the tonsure of the initiate.

Several points should be emphasized in this description. Note that there is not just one kind of gift. Some, as in the case of those given to the blacksmith and carpenter, are contractual, but are based on tradition rather than negotiated contracts, while other gifts are what we might call donations, and still others are traditional payments that are not explicitly calculated on the basis of the number of services performed. Even though we might say the system is a mixture of calculation and traditional payment, it is clearly not organized by the idea of calculation. Moreover, it is predominantly a religious system rather than an economic one.

As Hocart noted long ago, each jati has a priestly function and performs rituals that are necessary to the whole village (1950). The jajmani system is, as Hocart rightly argues, a sacrificial order. This is not an argument to the effect that the behavior of Indian villagers is totally without self-interest, but rather that self-interest is modulated by a kind of ritual structure similar to the one described in the classical sources. Individual self-interest is as prevalent in the Indian village as anywhere else, but it is neither the source of the structure nor the motive that makes it work.

Reciprocity and redistribution, however, are not the whole village story. Thought picture 3 represents a different situation, described also in the classical sources and even noted by Mauss. The giving of gifts (*dan*) is not always an exchange, but is, rather, a way of getting rid of inauspiciousness and ensuring well-being (Raheja 1988). As Raheja notes, inauspiciousness is the "poison" the giver wants to get rid of, much as we get rid of unwanted clothes when we donate them to charity. No return from the recipient is expected or wanted (thought picture 3). One can say that if there is a return in this case, it comes neither from the recipient nor as the result of a circulation of equivalent values.

Here, then, is the correction to Bataille, not in the sense of an economic surplus that must be wasted or redistributed, as in his understanding of the potlatch, but in the sense of getting rid of inauspiciousness. It is not that there is an excessive accumulation of inauspiciousness, but rather that the possibility of inauspiciousness is ever present and must be defended against—or, if contracted, must be gotten rid of by giving gifts.

In any event, circumstances in a peasant village have little to do with the idea of excess or surplus in the economic sense—lack is the common situation. Wasting a surplus production, then, has little relevance in this context, in either its economic or sacrificial sense. The dissipation of wealth or excess makes sense only where there is surplus to be wasted.

It is not so much the case that Bataille's construction offends against the sensibility of a restricted economy, but rather that it offends one's ecological sensibility. We could perhaps make use of Bataille's argument, though, if people could be convinced that wealth is inauspicious, something we need to get rid of or consume before it consumes us as we seek to pass through the eye of the needle.

Conclusion

Perhaps this discourse of the gift is a kind of detour that never returns to the main highway. Or maybe there is no main highway, and it's detour all the way. And perhaps, too, all my interest in the face-to-face and intentionality is a way of not facing up to the challenge of a faceless world in which intentions no longer belong to individuals, but are personified instead in interacting, abstract institutions that respond neither to my finite intentions nor to my finite calculations. This, however, may be too apocalyptic and ignores the fact that we all live in parallel realities, some of which may still respond, however fitfully, to our interests and intentions, while others may only appear to, and still others act on us in ways that are both beneath and beyond our comprehension.

Bibliography

Bourdieu, Pierre. 1990. *The Logic of Practice*. Trans. R. Nice. Cambridge: Polity Press.

Derrida, Jacques. 1992. *Given Time*. Trans. P. Kamuf. Chicago: University of Chicago Press.

Hocart, A. M. 1950. *Caste: A Comparative Study*. London: Methuen.

Newman, John, ed. 1999. *The Linguistics of Giving.* New York: John Benjamins Press.

Raheja, Gloria Goodwin. 1988. *The Poison in the Gift: Ritual, Prestation, and the Dominant Caste in a North Indian Village.* Chicago: University of Chicago Press.

Sahlins, Marshall. 1972. *Stone Age Economics.* Chicago: Aldine de Gruyter.

5

Mothering, Co-muni-cation, and the Gifts of Language

Genevieve Vaughan

"LOOK AT THE WORLD through women's eyes" was the motto of the United Nations NGO (Non-Governmental Organizations) conference in Huairou in 1995. Forty thousand women from all over the world attended the NGO conference. The critique of essentialism that is made by academic women's studies now makes us question whether there is any "point of view through women's eyes." This fact divides the women's movement for social change. I would like for this paper to help bridge that divide and show a direction in which women and men can move, both theoretically and practically, to solve the devastating problems caused by patriarchy and capitalism. The gift I am trying to give is not only academic but is directed toward social change.

Mothering is a practice called forth from adults by the biological dependency of infants. This dependence creates a social constant, in that someone must care for the children unilaterally for an extended period or they will not survive. Societies have ensured that adults will take on the care-giving role by assigning it to females and encouraging girls to imitate their mothers. It is the dependency of children that requires the intense care-giving activity, not the biology of the mothers. In fact, men could as easily engage in child care and some do, but males are usually given an identity and gender role whereby they are encouraged to be different from their nurturing mothers.

The values of patriarchy and capitalism combine to make us look at mothering through the wrong end of the telescope, relegating it to a very specific area of life disconnected from the rest— unmonetized, almost mindless, uninformative. Instead, the unilateral satisfaction of another's need that is necessary in mothering contains a basic recognizable logic, with many positive consequences. This logic functions prior to reciprocity and informs it. I call it "unilateral gift-giving," in order to emphasize its continuity with other kinds of gifts and exchanges, which I believe are actually variations on the theme of the unilateral gift.

By unilateral gift-giving I mean that, for example, a mother feeds her baby its lunch; the baby does not feed the mother lunch in return. (The transaction is, thus, at least deeply asymmetrical—the child may respond, but that does not transform the unilateral or unidirectional gift into an exchange.) From the child's point of view, she or he is the recipient of unilateral gift-giving coming from the other. This would be the case even if the adult were being paid to do the care giving.

Before I try to describe elements of the logic of the unilateral satisfaction of another's need, let me say that there is also a logic of commodity exchange for money that lays down a very strong base metaphor, or magnetic template, that influences us to interpret everything in its image. It is because of this strong pull toward the logic of exchange that we tend to ignore, discredit, or oversentimentalize unilateral gift-giving and overvalue exchange patterns. Exchange is a doubling of the gift but has the effect of canceling the motive and motion of the unilateral process. The generalization of exchange results in a very different configuration of human relations than would the generalization of unilateral gift-giving.

Since we are living in a society of "advanced" patriarchal capitalism in which commodity exchange for money is the order of the day, we are practicing exchange all the time and have become blind to the continued existence and importance of unilateral gift-giving. This blindness is also emotionally invested. It occurs in all areas of life and study, and it progresses from a denial of the existence of the unilateral-gift process to a denial of its validity, a knee-jerk delegitimation of gift-giving as instinctual, sentimental privilege, saintliness, or, at the other end of the spectrum, victimism or masochism.

The doubling of the gift in exchange forms the basis of a paradigm or worldview that opposes and cancels the values and views coming from the unilateral gift process.

Exchange, the process of giving in order to receive an equivalent, appears to contain a basic human logic of self-reflecting consciousness, self-respect, justice, fairness, equality. Quantification according to a monetary norm can be counted on to assess the even-handedness of transactions, so that all the parties seem to get what they gave and what they "deserve."

In Western culture, this pattern of interaction and its criteria are accepted as the normal human way of behaving, diminishing harm to the other while promoting the well-being of the self. From economics to politics, the idea of not impinging on the other rules over the idea of helping (giving to) the other. Feminists have embraced the idea of equality with men and shown that they can also embrace the values of patriarchal capitalism. While continuing to identify and give importance to needs, women do not usually consciously step outside the exchange paradigm. Instead they take up a struggle for rights within the system, rather than trying to change it altogether. One unchallenged patriarchal ideal, for example, is justice, which is based on the model of exchange, requires just payment for crime, and is now big business. The values of kindness, and the prevention of crime through the satisfaction of needs are not considered as relevant to the exchange-based discourse of justice and rights. The worldview or paradigm of exchange is actually conducting a continuous struggle against a hidden paradigm based on unilateral gift-giving, an (ideological) struggle that it is winning. We do not notice the gift paradigm or even know that it exists. Rather, we attribute isolated instances of unilateral giving to individual virtue, quirkiness, disguised self-interest or even codependency.

In this paper, I hope to provide a glimpse of what the world would look like if we restored unilateral gift-giving to its place as a core human logic, a theme upon which both symbolic gift exchange and commodity exchange are variations. I realize that using unilateral gift-giving as an interpretative key gives some very different perspectives on a number of issues. It is important to conceive of a different way in order to create it, to liberate it from its surroundings like the statue from the stone.

In fact I want to show that unilateral gift-giving is the basic mode of human interaction, and that half of humanity has been alienated from it by the imposition of the social construction of the male gender, thereby deeply altering also the circumstances and social construction of the gender of the other half of humanity.

If we can stand back and look at the exchange paradigm critically for a moment, we can begin to recognize the positive existence of the gift paradigm. The exchange paradigm has to dominate over the gift paradigm, because the gift paradigm threatens it by making it unnecessary. Indeed, if unilateral gift-giving were the norm, no one would need to exchange in order to receive what she or he needed. The exchange paradigm requires scarcity in order to maintain its leverage.

In capitalism, when abundance begins to accrue, scarcity is artificially created to save the exchange-based system. Agricultural products are plowed under in order to keep prices high. Money is spent on armaments and other waste and luxury items, or cornered in the hands of a few individuals or corporations, in order to create and maintain an appropriate climate of scarcity for business as usual to continue. These mechanisms have other advantages that also reward successful exchangers with social status and power and penalize gift givers by making their gift-giving (in scarcity) self-sacrificial.

A context of abundance would allow gift-giving to flower, while a context of scarcity discredits gift-giving by making it painfully difficult. Because of the conflict of paradigms and the tremendous real-world effects it has, it is not surprising that our individual views of the world have been deeply distorted. We are members of a society of advanced capitalism and have to succeed in it in order to survive, so that both women and men have adapted to the exchange paradigm and its values, allowing it to make us in its image. In everything we do, we are looking through the distorting glasses of exchange.

Nonetheless, through an effort of imagination, and because capitalism is destroying the gifts of the earth and humanity, we can also take the point of view of the gift paradigm. Women, who are still being brought up with the values that will allow them to do unilateral care giving, often maintain both paradigms internally, validating the exchange paradigm even while acting according to the values of the gift paradigm. It is important for all of us to resolve this contradiction and affirm that the gift paradigm is a valid way of viewing the world.

Indeed, I believe that the conflict between paradigms may be an important cause of misogyny. Women bear the brunt of the fact that the unilateral giving that they have to practice as mothers conflicts with and challenges the paradigm of exchange. In fact, because of the context of scarcity in which many mothers are forced to live, practicing the gift logic may even appear to be a punishment for not having succeeded in the system of commodity exchange. Alternatively, it may appear to be the reason for women's supposed "inferiority." Women themselves sometimes attribute the source of their oppression to the role of gift-giving rather than to the context of scarcity that has been created by the system based on commodity exchange. They think that by giving up gift-giving and convincing others to do so as well, they can improve their lot. Instead, the solution is to change the context of scarcity and the economic system that is causing it, so as to make gift-giving viable for all.

The conflicts of values that many people, both women and men, have regarding patriarchal capitalism are usually seen as individual propensities, not as the values of a different hidden vestigial or incipient system. By giving positive attention to unilateral gift-giving, we can begin to recognize its social importance.

One result of the predominance of the exchange paradigm is that needs have become invisible, unless their satisfaction is backed by the money required to pay for them as "effective demand." Looking beyond the exchange paradigm to a theory of gift-giving as need, satisfaction would also require an expanded visibility of needs to include those for which the people who experience them do not have the wherewithal, as well as those needs which are not part of the monetized economy.

Marx's discussion of consumptive production and productive consumption could be used as the basis for such a theory, since it suggests how needs can become specific and diversify according to the means by which they are satisfied (Marx 1973, 90–94). New needs arise on the basis of the satisfaction of the old in a dynamic way. For example, a child who first needs only milk begins to also require solid foods, prepared with specific cultural procedures, and so on. A child who was dependent begins to need independence. The gift process in coexistence with exchange gives rise to many needs. As adults living in the exchange paradigm, we have complex social and psychological needs having to do with power relations. For example, the need to be respected may be more important than the need to receive a gift. Much damage has been done by givers who paternalistically ignore the variety of needs and the creativity of the receiver.

The concealment of the gift paradigm has extended to our terminology, rendering the gifts we are already giving invisible. For example, we place the neutral term *activity* over the loaded term *gift* in many aspects of life. At the same time, we have taken away the loaded term *satisfaction of need* and replaced it with *effect*. Building (or taking care of) a house can be considered as satisfying a complex combination of needs by as many activities. I propose that in order to reveal the gift paradigm, we reconsider even those activities according to the theme of unilateral gift-giving and receiving.

Aspects of the Gift Logic

The process of unilateral gift-giving as evidenced in nurturing has its own logic, with consequences and implications. I will list some of the aspects of this logic as I see them.

One: The gift interaction requires the giver's ability to recognize needs of others and to procure or fashion something to satisfy them. The satisfaction of needs is not done by humans ahistorically, but always takes place at a certain cultural and historical level with the means and methods that are present in the society at a certain degree of development of productive forces, and within some mode of production. Thus, whatever is received in satisfaction of a need is formed with some degree of cultural specificity that also educates further needs.

Two: The gift interaction has three parts: the giver, the gift or service, and the receiver with her/his need. Leaving out the receiver as an important element in this process would make us look at gift-giving as an ego-based process, done for the good of the giver, as happens in exchange. The transitivity of the gift process depends upon the reception and use of the gift by the receiver.

Three: A dynamic change of state occurs in which the giver is first in possession of the gift, then she gives it, and finally the gift comes to rest in the possession of or incorporated into the body of the receiver. This is a transitive interaction.

Four: The purpose of the gift is the satisfaction of the need and well-being of the receiver. The interaction is other-oriented.

Five: Giving a gift to satisfy another's need gives value to that person, because the implication is that if that person were not valuable to the giver, s/he would not have given the gift. This has the effect that attention goes to the (valuable) receiver rather than to the giver. The giver can satisfy a receiver's need to be valued by giving to her and can modify and intensify that value by self-effacing (self-sacrifice). A further variation is that the receiver can refuse to recognize the giver as the source of the gift, as if the value and the gift came from herself or himself through deserving.

Six: The receiver is not passive but creative. The gift must be used in order for the transaction to be complete.

Seven: Gift-giving creates a bond between giver and receiver. The giver recognizes the existence and needs of the other, then fashions or provides something specific to satisfy those needs. She is assured of the reception of the gift by the well-being of the other. The receiver finds that her need has been satisfied in a specific way by another, with something that she did not procure herself. These two poles can be seen as the basis of interpersonal bonds. The receiver can recognize the positive existence of the other. Potentially she can also experience gratitude, a response by which she celebrates the gift she has received. She can become a giver in her turn.

Eight: Turn-taking occurs when individuals give unilateral gifts sequentially, without intending to cause the receiver to give an equivalent in return.

Nine: These gift processes also constitute the subject as a giver and/or creative receiver. The body itself is both a product and a source of gifts (different from the subject of exchange, where debt and reciprocity are necessary).

Ten: There is logical consequence in gift-giving, as in "if A gives to B and B gives to C, then A gives to C" (B is then mediator between A and C).

This list is not meant to be comprehensive, but only to bring forward several aspects of unilateral gift-giving, including the relation-making capacity of unilateral other-oriented gift-giving; the informative capacity of satisfying needs and, thus, of educating them; the implication of value of the other; and the creativity of the receivers. No debt or obligation to reciprocate is necessary for the formation of interpersonal bonds through gift-giving.

In fact, I believe that there are several reasons why we have focused so much on the relations created by the obligations of reciprocity. For now I will mention two. As I said above, we are looking from the perspective of capitalism, where reciprocity is enforced as the mechanism of market exchange and debt is a salient factor of the economy. Second, gift-giving is labile, mercurial, and can easily switch before our eyes from unilateral to bilateral. An other-oriented gift can transform into an ego-oriented one simply by instrumentalizing the gift to satisfy the needs of the original giver.

When this happens, we sometimes summon our cynicism and decide that the free gift was an illusion. We say "there is no free lunch," forgetting that women have been cooking lunch for free for millennia. Manipulation through gift-giving is always possible, through leveraging gifts, giving competitively, withholding gifts. The exchange paradigm continually pushes us in that direction. We use this tendency of gift-giving to transform itself as evidence that unilateral gift-giving does not exist. Mothers, and other people who have done a lot of gift-giving on a daily basis, know that it does.

Despite this unfortunate tendency, the unilateral gift continues to function in the area of mothering, and it has also many developments that have been attributed to other aspects of life and been given other names. By restoring the name *gift* to the developments in other aspects of life, we can see that unilateral gift-giving is one of the load-bearing structures of society and not just wishful thinking or a good intention transformed into its opposite.

If we consider the movement of goods and services provided by care givers to needs of children and other family members as unilateral gift-giving, we can also see that gift-giving in large part forms the material bodies of the people in the community. I would call this "material nonsign communication." It is a transfer of gifts from one person to another by which the bodies and minds of persons grow and become specific, due to the fact that needs become specified or educated by what satisfies them. It is no wonder that the words *co-muni-cation* and *co-muni-ty* can remind us of the process of giving gifts together. By giving unilaterally and receiving gifts from others, we mutually include each other with regard to all the parts of our environment.

It is only because mothering has been so misunderstood and problematized in our own society that we have not been able to see the processes it provides as having a continuity with the rest of life. Denied this continuity, nurturing appears to be and becomes even more specialistic and limited, carrying the domestic sphere into some unconscious never-never land upon which consumerism and advertising nevertheless feed. Exchange is self-reflecting and self-validating, difficult to oppose. However, if we look at unilateral gift-giving as the core process from which both symbolic gift exchange and commodity exchange derive, we can reintegrate mothering into the rest of life, and childhood along with it.

We can find the continuity between capitalist and precapitalist societies. By giving value to the gift-giving process, we will also be able to recognize the nonmetaphorical aspects of the idea of Gaia, our Mother Earth. If we can reactivate the attitudes of creative receiving that we used as children in our experience of gift-giving and receiving, rather than covering them with a neutrality deriving from the exchange paradigm, we can rebirth our gratitude for life and for the abundant planet on which we live, and that we are now destroying because we are caught in the egocentrism and solipsism of the exchange paradigm.

Exchange Relations

Exchange is giving in order to receive an equivalent. It requires a return gift, which is determined by the value of what has been given. The exchange of commodities requires measurement, quantification, and assessment in money. Exchange is ego-oriented. The need that is satisfied by exchange is the exchanger's own need. Therefore it does not attribute value to the other, but only to the self. Commodity exchange for money mediates generalized private property, where all property is owned in a mutually exclusive way by private owners. Exchange is adversarial, in that in each transaction each person is trying to get more and give less. Exchange does not establish human relations beyond those of mutual equality as exchangers. (In fact, we will see that this equality is an illusion, because many exchangers are receiving free gifts covered by the equality of the exchange, and many others are giving free gifts because the "just" price covers a source of free gifts.)

As a template or deep metaphor for other interactions, exchange is very powerful. The self-reflecting aspect in the equation of value (x commodity = y amount of money) creates an artificial standard for what humans are and what their relations should be. We think of consciousness as self-reflection, and we appeal to relations of equality, balance, and justice. These seemingly positive qualities function in the mode of exchange, but by accepting them our way is blocked to the higher goods of unilateral gift-giving: celebrating qualitative difference, caring, mutual imbalance toward the other, attention to needs, and kindness rather than justice.

Psychological Origins of Exchange

Nancy Chodorow and other feminist psychoanalysts discuss the plight of the boy child who finds he has to learn or invent an identity that is not like that of his nurturing mother (Chodorow 1978; Pollack 1998). The boy begins life without knowing he is different. Then he discovers that he has a different gender name, and thus belongs to a different category. But if, as I am saying, the fundamental unilateral gift-giving that is happening and through which he is bonding with his mother is interpreted as a female characteristic only, where does that leave the boy? What can his identity be? Society has interpreted our physiological differences to mean that we must construct different gender identities, but if the unilateral gift-giving way is the core process, what other identity can there be for the boy?

I believe naming has a lot to do with this identity—that the word *male* itself (in its binary opposition to *female*) categorizes the boy and provides a model of categorization and alienation that has widespread repercussions. By taking the father or other important male as the model or prototype of the human, the boy is consoled for his departure from the nurturing category. The mother is then seen as not the prototype for *human,* her nurturing appears to be of little value, and her status appears inferior to the boy's. In fact, she appears to nurture males more because they are not nurturers.

Males then vie with each other to be the prototype (male) human, while women are in a category that nurtures them and that is "inferior" because women do not vie to be the prototype. The "essence" of women appears to be that they are not even in the running. The fact that the contest is artificial and unnecessary does not diminish its social significance for everyone.

If almost everything that little children have is, or seems to be, a gift from their mothers, the penis would also seem to be a gift, given to boys but not to girls. It could appear that the boy has been put in the nonnurturing superior category because he has it. Yet because the identity constructed through the gift way with the mother is necessarily more satisfying than an identity of similarity with the father—where he has to compete to be the prototype—he still longs for participation in the gift mode.

But since the mother doesn't have a penis and the boy's gender appears to be determined by his having one, castration seems to be the way to return to the nurturing identity, and he would desire it. At the same time he would necessarily fear castration, making the whole issue very traumatic. (Also the fact that the boy will never have breasts, though he may envy them as the gift of nurturing, would enter into this psychological pattern as well. Thus, it seems that the mother is in the opposite and inferior category because she has the gift of breasts for nurturing, which he does not have.)

The boy therefore puts himself out of dependent receivership of the cares of the mother and begins to feel that he deserves such care, because of the gift of his penis and his name. He sees himself as made or engendered by the father, who traveled the same psychological itinerary himself, as a child. I believe this childhood pattern repeats itself in many areas of social life in the creation of privileged categories by naming, based on the naming of gender.

The privilege involved is the direction of gifts and services by others "upward" toward the person who is in the superior category, and the giving of names and commands "downward" by the person in the superior category. In this way hierarchies are created, and those with important titles in top places—prototype positions—rule with their phallic symbols in hand. From the scepter to the miter to the missile and the gun, our leaders are made male again and again.

The division into genders due to our physiological differences is an easy mistake for cultures to make. In fact, we put things that look different into different categories. The problem is that humans are so sensitive and intelligent that they take up their categories and use them as self-fulfilling prophecies. This very capacity, however, would also give us a way out, an ability to create ourselves differently. We could undo the categories and change gender expectations.

The transfer of categories away from nurturing and into a relation of similarity and competition with the father is remarkably similar to the change of a product from a use value to an exchange value. The product is taken away from the production process (which could be viewed as a combination of need-satisfying activities), placed on the market (the binary opposite of gift-giving), compared to the monetary norm, and given a "money name," a price. Marx makes a comparison between price and proper names and adds, "We know nothing of a man simply because he is called 'James' " (1930, 77). I have to differ with Marx. We do know that if he is called James he is male.

Girls travel more slowly, remaining like their mothers in the gift realm. But they too are given up at last, renamed, and placed in a new family category with its prototypical male, the husband toward whom they will direct their gift-giving. Commodity exchange that cancels the gift, requiring an equivalent, seems to do the trick of nurturing while not nurturing, satisfying needs while competing to have more, making it an apparently ungendered area more appropriate for masculine endeavor.

MANHOOD SCRIPT

According to David Gilmore in his book *Manhood in the Making* (1990), the values males embrace for the formation of their identities can be seen as having to do with a "manhood script" that is relatively similar cross-culturally. Such values as independence, competitiveness, performative excellence, courage, and large size form the parameters of this script, which is embraced and constructed by males so as to distinguish themselves from the nurturing mother. I think we can recognize that these values are similar to the values of capitalism: autonomy, competitiveness, performative excellence, risk taking, and high status due to social "size": having more wealth or power.

Having given up unilateral gift-giving as both a gender and a mode of production and distribution, it appears that it is only through the rule of law or the strictures of morality and religion that men (and women living in capitalism) can be convinced to pay attention to others' needs. Yet self-interest is a psychological dead end. People find their lives without "meaning." Searching for meaning individually is an almost impossible task, since in both language and life meaning has to do with communication, with orientation toward the other.

We seize upon the law of the male prototype as the measure of our behavior, but this does not bring us back to the gift way, which seems an impossible, unrealistic Eden. Meanwhile the economic way of the manhood script continues to make an anti-Eden, creating poverty where abundance should be, rewarding the few with ever-greater havings while penalizing the many, erecting a wall behind which the gift-giving garden is no longer visible.

One advantage that capitalism has had, the silver lining of its cloud, is that by institutionalizing the values of the manhood script and bringing women into the monetized labor force, it has shown that those supposedly male values were not biologically based, given that women can embrace them successfully as well. A society based on unilateral gift-giving, institutionalizing the script of nurturing, would show that those processes and values are not limited to biological females.

LANGUAGE

One attempt that we can make to institutionalize nurturing is to reveal it in areas of life where it has been canceled and made invisible by the paradigm of exchange. I believe that we need to re-envision language itself as an ideal gift economy. As such, it can function as the missing link between mothering, symbolic gift exchanges, and commodity exchange. In my book *For-Giving: A Feminist Criticism of Exchange,* and in some early essays, I suggest that language can be conceived of as a construction of unilateral gift processes, taking its communicative power from the ability gift-giving has to create relations (Vaughan 1997). Words would thus be verbal gifts that substitute for co-muni-cative gifts, which humans give to one another to satisfy communicative needs— needs for a relation and for a means for creating that relation regarding something.

Unmotivated phonemes and morphemes are combined to make up word-gifts that become common possessions of a community. Word-gifts are made on purpose to create relations, to satisfy communicative needs, not to direct material needs. They are put by individuals into contingent so-called "rule-governed" combinations, creating momentary present-time common relations among interlocutors regarding the many aspects of the human and natural environment. Even the "rules of syntax" by which the word-gifts are combined with each other can be viewed as transposed gift processes.

If it is possible to create a mutually inclusive relation with someone by satisfying her need with a material object, we can also give that gift in order to create that relation. However, need-satisfying objects are not always available, and there are many parts of the world we cannot use to satisfy needs directly. Thus we use words, verbal gifts, to satisfy others' communicative needs for a means to create a relation to something. The speaker or giver recognizes the listener's lack of a relation to something in the present and speaks or gives the word that has become the general social substitute gift for that kind of thing in her culture.

By combining constant word-gifts, she is able to make a contingent word-gift: a sentence, or group of sentences, that expresses the specific relevance of the kind of things in the moment. By satisfying the other's need for a means to a relation, the speaker has satisfied her own need for a common relation with the listener in the present. The listener's relation to the means of communication the speaker has given her is at the same time the speaker's own shared relation with the listener. She has created a mutually inclusive relation with another person regarding a thing or kind of thing, by means of combined word-gifts. The listener or receiver has to be able to creatively use what has been given to her, or the relation is not established.

According to Marx's idea from the *German Ideology,* language is "practical consciousness that exists for others and therefore really for me as well" (Engels and Marx 1964, 21). What the word-gift is for the speaker is determined by what it is for the listener. The use of the gift by the receiver is as important to the transaction as the giving of the gift by the giver. In fact, if we want to communicate, we have to speak in a language the listener understands. If even one word is unknown to her, we have to define or contextualize it or simply give her a different one.

Syntax

I think that even syntax can be viewed as transposed gift-giving. I started out by saying that the unilateral gift process has at least three parts: a giver, a gift or service, and a receiver with a need. In old-fashioned grammar terms, these would correspond to subject, predicate, and object. In more current terms, we would say that the relation "noun phrase + verb phrase" is a gift relation. The plus sign stands for a unity between the two, created by a transposed gift relation. In "The blonde girl hit the ball," we give the word *blonde* to the word *girl* because the girl is seen as having that property. She has it because it was given to her on the reality plane, and we are able to say it because we are giving one word to the other word on the verbal plane. The word *the* is an article that can be given to the word *girl* because *girl* is a noun, the kind of word that can receive and use the gift of the article *the*. The adjective *blonde* is also the kind of word-gift that can be given to a noun.

In fact, on the reality plane, only certain kinds of gifts can be given and received by certain people. "The blonde girl" constitutes the subject of the sentence, the transposed giver. The verb *hit* is the transposed gift and *the ball* the transposed receiver. When the sentence is made passive, the emphasis is on the reception of the gift: "The ball was hit by the blonde girl." I can only briefly sketch here what could be an alternative feminist approach to the understanding of language. What I want to suggest, however, is the deep information-bearing capacity of the gift relation. I do believe it would be possible to translate language analysis back into gift terms.

I think there are two aspects of language corresponding very roughly to Saussure's *langue-parole* distinction. The langue side comes from naming and the definition, while the parole side comes from the use of the words we have gained through naming and definition, and through participating in speech interaction. I think that exchange corresponds to the naming and definition (langue) side of this distinction, while unilateral gift-giving corresponds to the use of words, sentences, discourses.

We usually tend to confuse the two, not realizing that definition has a structure and implications that are different from nondefinitional sentences. Thus we believe that by putting things in categories, seeing what they are like or unlike, and what the categories include or exclude, we understand them. By concentrating on categorization, we are leaving out the gift motivation and communicative power that could explain how language is connected to the extralinguistic world and how people are connected to each other. The definition is actually a metalinguistic gift, while language in context functions as a linguistic gift satisfying ongoing and contingent communicative needs.

Communicative needs arise with regard to all parts of our environment, and with regard to some parts more often and more constantly than others. Thus we have socially invented some means that arise as constants (each of which is a variable regarding the others), and we combine them in a contingent and fleeting relation to each other, to which we relate parts of the environment in the moment. Our interpersonal relations acquire a specificity regarding each kind of thing as mediated by the constants that are assembled in ever-new combinations, according to the relevance to each other of things to which we respond in our ongoing experience. We can also consider the verbal gifts we are giving as having value, and we can construct other gift combinations in the present, forming still other relations with the listener in their regard. The listener can, in turn, contribute her gifts.

In language the lexicon constitutes a basic abundant supply of word-gifts (the constants), a competence that members of a community all possess (specialistic and elite languages, of course, exist, but I am trying to describe the basic case). This supply provides people with a situation of common possession of linguistic means of production. Due to the facility with which we speak, we are in the position of having a limitless supply of gifts to give. We are also in the position of producing for others what they could potentially rather easily produce for themselves.

This abundance and ease contrasts with the scarcity and the difficulty of procuring and giving gifts in the extralinguistic world. Communicative needs may appear much less stringent and compelling than material needs. Nevertheless, verbal communication can have a use value regarding the satisfaction of material needs, because humans can use the gifts they receive from it as information upon which to base their behavior. Verbal communication, thus, has a gift value that creates human relations with regard to things, as well as a use value—which arises from our ability to use these relations as the premise upon which to base further behavior, relations, and interactions.

For example, if I say "The book is on the table," your communicative needs are satisfied for the moment, and I have satisfied your need to know where the book is. I may have saved you an hour of time looking for the book. Whether or not you asked me, I have unilaterally satisfied your need. My sentence has a use value and also a gift value, because I use it to satisfy your communicative need and your extralinguistic need for finding the book, both of which give value to you by implication.

In the definition, we are taking words out of context and looking at them as constants. The process in the definition is much like that of exchange, in that it is based on the substitution of equivalents. In the definition, the definiens is substituted by the definiendum. The gift of a "new" word, the definiendum, is given to the listener. Similarly, in exchange the commodity is substituted by money, which can be used again to take the place of another commodity of similar value. There are important differences, of course.

Because money mediates the exchange of mutually exclusive private property and it is not infinitely reproducible like words, it is given up as property in exchange for the commodity. Word-gifts can be used again and again, and they mediate human relations of mutual inclusion and community rather than the relations of mutual exclusion and the market. They provide an infinite qualitative variety of relations to the world, while money only mediates one relation, the exchange of property, in quantitative variety according to its standard.

The infinite variety of qualitatively different relations that humans create with each other through language regarding things has had an important gift value for the human community. The cultural environment that humans have made for themselves has been deeply altered by the contributions of verbal communication. Straw mats and tables, gardens and factories would not be there if humans had not had language. The natural environment has acquired new gift characteristics that depend in part upon the ability of the collective to respond to the environment with their verbal gifts and their verbally mediated interactions.

Even more distant parts of nature become gifts to us because we alter our response in their regard, and this alteration requires the use of language. While the moon remains relatively untouched by humans, the kind of gift it is for us has changed over the centuries and cross-culturally, because we alter our response to it through ritual and through science, through astrology and astronomy. In all of these endeavors language has contributed a use value, in that it has served to create human interpersonal, individual, and collective relations to the world. And it has had a gift value, implying the value of people and cultures.

Unilateral gift-giving is transitive. By satisfying a need, we give value to the other and to the need. In so doing we create ourselves as giving and receiving subjectivities. In speaking to someone about something we also give value to that person, to the part of the environment with regard to which we have satisfied her communicative need and to the means of communication we have used. In this way we also create ourselves as subjects, linguistic givers and receivers of verbal gifts and value. We continue to give and receive verbally even when we are not giving gifts materially.

We can create our subjectivities as linguistic givers and receivers even when we are mainly subjects immersed in commodity production and exchange, exploitation, violence, and war. Language can be used to dominate and manipulate others just as material gift-giving can. However, the basic transitive logics of both language and material gift-giving function because they create positive co-muni-tary human relations and the material and psychological subjectivities of the members of the community.

There are some aspects of language that seem to be reincarnated in gift exchange. For example giving the return gift of the "same thing" in gift exchange, a practice discussed by Godelier, could be interpreted as functionally analogous to language, where speakers of the same language possess and are able to combine, give, and receive the normatively identical words, demonstrating that they belong to the same community (Godelier 1996). The need in gift "exchange" to reciprocate with something more than the original gift shows that at least that extra portion of it is unilateral and free. In fact, the exchange of gifts could be seen as material dialogue (with some of the same agonistic potential as verbal dialogue).

The process of substitution of one gift for another itself creates a new area of gift-giving, with new consequences. It has been said that gift exchange is different from language, because gifts are not referential. Substitute gifts, however, can be referential. They can bring us back, remind us of the gifts they have taken the place of. In gift exchange, not only are the human interactions structured in a similar way, with the second gift transaction reversing the first, but the relation between the two gifts is affirmed by their similarity, so that the act of giving the return gift refers to the original gift (by repeating it).

Beyond this reference, the addition of "more" places the new giver in the position of giving unilaterally again. Thus, gift exchanges might be seen as occupying a communicative position somewhere *between* unilateral gift-giving and language proper. I believe this may have happened because language itself is functioning as a deep metaphor upon which humans base other behaviors, not only regarding structures deriving from the relations in Saussure's langue, as Lévi-Strauss showed, but in the sense of a parole that is based on satisfying communicative needs through gift-giving and from which langue, which is, after all, an abstraction, derives.

As I have been saying, I believe that living in a society based on the exchange paradigm prevents us from seeing the gift-giving that is before us. Exchange value appears to be the most important kind, different from other kinds of values—moral, linguistic, spiritual values, and so on. Indeed, exchange value can be seen as a transformation of (unilateral) gift value, canceling and hiding it. In fact, it is the single-minded concentration on the need of the giver rather than the receiver that cancels the transitivity (inclusiveness, creativity, transmission of a variety of qualitative values) of the gift transformed by exchange.

Exchange value is the value of the need-satisfying product—the ex-gift or would-be gift—for others in the system of alienated mutually exclusive co-muni-cation that is the exchange of private property. After the commodity has passed through the market, its use value has had gift value deleted from it because, in fact, the gift value was transitive (implying the value of the other). The product that has been exchanged on the market does not give value to the buyer beyond what she or he originally gave. In fact, in a mediated way the buyer has given it to her or himself.

There are many other characteristics that separate language as a verbal gift economy from material gift-giving. I will not go in to them here. I just want to mention, though, that I think it is possible that if we were living in material abundance and doing generalized unilateral gift-giving, new, unexpected results would arise from those relations, social epiphenomena by which our communities would be empowered and our collective artistic and spiritual abilities enhanced.

The fact that gifts-in-exchange have been used agonistically or in status-conferring ways has more to do with different modes of patriarchy than with the logic of unilateral gift-giving itself. The patriarchal exchange paradigm (and the "manhood script") has blocked the development of the gift paradigm in many different ways, and thereby has deeply alienated and altered our human potential, preventing the (spiritual, economic, and cultural) evolution of both women and men.

Marx's semiotics of the market gives us the clue for a semiotics of the unilateral gift, of language, and of gift exchange. All of these areas have to do with human value-conferring activity, activity for others and therefore for oneself (again according to Marx's dialectic of linguistic inclusion from the *German Ideology*), gift-giving, the activity of satisfying needs at different levels. If we consider the process of commodity exchange a descendant of language (in its aspects of definition and naming), and language itself a descendant of gift-giving, we can understand different kinds of value as variations upon a single theme. Commodity exchange, gift exchange, language, and unilateral gift-giving continue to coexist, however, and reciprocally influence each other. They are difficult to disentangle. By giving attention to unilateral gift-giving, we can uncover it in many areas where it is called something else or where it is mixed in with exchange.

Marx believed the capitalists' profit came from surplus value, the part of the value of labor not covered by the workers' salary. This unpaid labor can be considered a (leveraged) gift from the worker to the capitalist. Recognizing the gift element in profit reveals that the gift is the motivating element of the whole system. The exchange economy is sustained by gifts in other ways. The housewife's free labor is a gift to the market system. It has been calculated that if housework were monetized, some 40 percent would have to be added to the gross national product in the U.S., more in some other countries. This unilateral gift is transitive, passing through the household and the salaried worker to the capitalist, giving value to the system itself and providing its validation.

Free gifts travel upward in hierarchies, bearing with them the implication of value and power of those above over those below, while those at the top use some of the gifts they receive to pay for the creation of other hierarchies of constraint, such as police or military, so that the direction of the flow of gifts upward can be maintained. Countries of the Global South give and give way to the countries of the North, nurturing them with hidden gifts of all kinds. The flow of gifts goes away from those with the needs toward those in the hierarchies in the South and toward those in the hierarchies in the North, who have invested there for their own so-called "just profit." The flow of gifts goes upward away from the needs, also from the earth into the hands of the few, away from the needs of the many in the present and in the future, who will not be able to sustain themselves and their children with the toxic soil and polluted air we are presently creating.

Those of us who are to any extent the beneficiaries of this transfer of abundance should creatively receive it, to try to devise ways to peacefully change the system of exploitation. We can begin by creating a "translation" that will revalidate unilateral gift-giving as the basis of communication and community, and stop validating the universalization of the practice, categories, and values of exchange. Communication and economics appear to be completely different things, because they are located in different categories. Yet the enigma of the gift and the enigma of the commodity can both be unraveled by studying economics as co-muni-cation. Language, gender, gift-giving, and exchange all continue to be made enigmatic by the cancellation of the mother and unilateral gift-giving.

Looking at the world through women's eyes means resolving these enigmas, approaching our lives with the sure knowledge that the kind of unilateral gift logic we learned from our mothers is not an isolated propensity to nurture, secondary in importance to the values of the manhood script, but rather is the basis of the way we all form ourselves and each other as humans. It is exchange, the doubling back of the gift upon the giver that obscures the truth and creates the many problems to be solved. We are living in a pathological system. The solutions that the system proposes only aggravate the problems. We need to base a new cure on a new diagnosis.

I believe the disease is patriarchal capitalism. The cure can begin by giving value to unilateral gift-giving.

BIBLIOGRAPHY

Chodorow, Nancy. 1978. *The Reproduction of Mothering.* Berkeley and Los Angeles: University of California Press.

Engels, Friedrich, and Karl Marx. 1964. *The German Ideology.* Progress Publishers, Moscow.

Gilmore, David D. 1990. *Manhood in the Making.* New Haven and London: Yale University Press.

Godelier, Maurice. 1996. *L'enigme du don.* Fayard.

Marx, Karl. 1973. *Grundrisse.* Trans. Martin Nicolaus. New York: Vintage Books.

———. 1930. *Capital.* 2 vols. London: J. M. Dent and Sons.

Pollack, William. 1998. *Real Boys.* New York: Random House.

Vaughan, Genevieve. 1997. *For-Giving, a Feminist Criticism of Exchange.* Austin, Tex.: Plain View Press.

3

The Gift of Philosophical Discourse

6

The Time of Giving, the Time of Forgiving

John D. Caputo

The Aporia of Forgiveness

The "logic" of forgiveness reproduces the paradox of the gift. The very conditions that make forgiveness possible also make it impossible. For if forgiveness is to be forgiveness, it must be a gift, namely the gift in which I give away the debt you owe me, the *for* in *forgive*, having the sense of "away" or "forth." That is why, when someone owes us something, we say we "have something on them" or, even more brutally, "have them," which means that in forgiveness, I give up what I have on the other. I release them and let them go.

Now if forgiveness is to be a gift, it seems it must be unconditional. If the other is to be forgiven only after measuring up to certain conditions, if the other must earn or deserve forgiveness, then to forgive him is to give him just what he has earned, to give him his fair wages. That would not be to give a gift, but to give the other his due, to repay his repentance with the wages of forgiveness; it would be not a gift but the economy of retributive justice. As Derrida asks: "And does one have to deserve forgiveness? One may deserve an excuse, but ought not forgiveness be accorded without regard to worthiness? Ought not a true forgiveness (a forgiveness in authentic money) absolve the fault or the crime even as the fault and the crime remain what they are?" (1992, 163).

But in the great religious traditions, in both Jewish and Christian theology, forgiveness always functions as an economy, where it is regulated by a certain calculus, by a calculated set of conditions: the offender must confess the wrong that was done, feel contrite and sad about it, make every effort at restitution that circumstances permit, and finally resolve to offend no more. If the other has met all those conditions, then the other deserves and is owed forgiveness, and we no longer "have" anything on the other. The repentant deserves forgiveness the way a man who has paid off his mortgage deserves the title to the property.

That means that conditional forgiveness is less a gift than an economic exchange: forgiveness is exchanged for repentance. That is the economy of forgiveness, and it makes perfect sense, but it is not a gift. Everything remains with the realm of being and presence and the principle of sufficient reason. But the gift should be bound only by goodness, not being; the gift needs only to be as good as it can be, and it need not have a sufficient reason for being.

Forgiveness is possible as a gift only if it is unconditional, for as soon as the offender meets the required conditions, then it is no longer forgiveness but a fair exchange, and it would be positively unjust not to forgive the offender. But by enforcing these conditions, which are only reasonable, it is clear that we forgive only those who are no longer offending, who have had a change of heart (*metanoia*) and made restitution as far as possible. Yet unconditional forgiveness looks like madness, for that would imply that one could only forgive someone who is still offending, who does not deserve it, who has not earned it, but upon whom it is bestowed "graciously" or, should we say, gratuitously.

We would forgive those who are guilty and unrepentant and who have no intention, now or in the future, of making restitution or of sinning no more. Unconditional forgiveness would come down to the madness of forgiving sinners, to forgiving sinners qua sinners, just insofar as they are sinners, while they are still sinning.

Now while the idea of forgiving sinners is a well-known and quite venerable idea, it does appear to be utterly mad and, in the sense we are describing here, actually to have been more or less rejected by both the theological and philosophical traditions. We all agree that forgiveness is for sinners, but by "sinners" we usually mean those who intend to sin no more, reformed sinners, former sinners. If we mean people who are sinners and are still sinning, with no intention of ceasing their sin, then it appears unreasonable or mad to forgive them, because they do not deserve it. Is forgiveness for those who are no longer sinners, or is it for sinners, for those who are still sinners?

It would be unfair not to forgive those who deserve it, and it would be mad to forgive those who do not. But if forgiving is a gift, if we give without return and are not simply giving back to the repentant sinner what he has earned and deserves, then it is the sinner qua sinner, the sinner who is still sinning, whom we must forgive—who, in a certain sense, is the only one we can forgive if forgiveness is a gift and not an exchange. Unconditional forgiveness would institute a kind of special alliance between God and sinners. This concept makes religion, although it says it is for sinners, very nervous, even as it makes the philosophers very nervous, for they are loathe to do things without a sufficient reason.

In actual practice, forgiveness is reserved for non-sinners, while the sinners can go to the devil unless and until they shape up and stop sinning. We forgive non-sinners, who have earned it, for whom it is a supplement or a complement (or compliment), but not sinners, who really need it. Matthew has Jesus say, very astutely I think, that just as physicians are for the sick, not the healthy, forgiveness is for the sinners, not the righteous (Matt. 2:17). But in actual practice, the logic of forgiveness looks a lot like the logic of banking: the bankers make loans only to those who have good credit and can offer the bank a security, whereas the truly destitute, who really need a loan, can never get one because they are a credit risk.

Bankers lend money to people who have money, not to people who do not. That is because bankers are not into gifts, and when a bank offers to give you a gift, watch out: they are only after your business, the proof of which is that if afterward you miss a payment, they will not easily forgive you. True gifts and radical forgiveness are not good business. Giving and forgiving, if there are such things, do not make for good banking (or good ecclesiology).

We might try to dodge this bullet by saying—and this is a famous axiom of the logic of forgiveness—that we forgive the sinner but not the sin. Now while that is better than not forgiving either one, it too remains something conditional and less than the gift of full forgiveness. We are letting ourselves off easy. I forgive you,

but not what you have done. But what is a sin? It is a sinner sinning, a concrete, factical deed, datable in time, locatable in space.
It is not some abstract, ethics-book definition of something evil,
of murder or oppression, say, that politicians and other people
in love with their own rhetoric but with no taste for action can
sanctimoniously denounce. It is a concrete murder, which requires a concrete murderer, who is built right into the definition.

And what are sinners? Sinners are, in an important sense, the
sum of their deeds. You cannot separate the doer and the deed,
as a famous antimoralist once said. In the moment of sinning, the
sinner and the sin are one. So to forgive the sinner and not the
sin is to forgive the sinner up to a point, but no further. It is to
forgive that part of the sinner that did not sin in the past and will
not sin in the future, but not that part of the sinner that has been
sinning and so needs forgiveness. I do not forgive you in those
moments of your life where you were or are still sinning or are
planning to sin some more. So once again, I am not forgiving
sinning, which needs forgiveness, but not non-sinning, which
does not. I do not forgive that part of you that has done this, and
if you do it again, if you revisit me again with this part of you that
I don't forgive, then I may call whole deal off. If I forgive the doer
but not the deed, the offender but not the offense, then I am
inserting an important condition into my forgiveness, which gives
every appearance of being a very tentative and conditional ar-
rangement.

THE PHARISEE AND THE TAX COLLECTOR

The scriptural accounts of the forgiveness of sins are a rich re-
source for gaining some clarity on these matters, particularly as
regards the question of unconditional forgiveness: for God, as the
bountiful source of all good gifts, ought to be above all a bountiful source of mercy and forgiveness. Let us turn to the well-known
story in the gospel of Luke (18:9–14) in which a Pharisee and a
tax collector—a Jew who collaborates with the Romans by collect-
ing Roman taxes from his fellow Jews—go up to the temple to
pray. The Pharisee thanks God that he is not like everybody else,
like the adulterers and thieves, and especially not like this tax

collector. The tax collector, on the other hand, cannot so much as lift his head, but simply says, "God have mercy on me, sinner that I am." We can hardly fail to grasp the point of this story about vaulting moral pride and a lowly, touching humility.

But let us consider a more radical rendering of this parable suggested by A. N. Wilson (1992, 30–31). He claims that the story goes back to an older pre-Lucan source, and that Luke has misunderstood the story—which is possible, unless the story is of Luke's own devising, which is also possible (Sanders 1985, 175; 385 n. 6).

We get a better picture of the supposed original story by taking two crucial steps: (1) We should remember that by the end of the first century, the Pharisees have become a focal point of the Christian struggle against the Jewish establishment, and that the historical Pharisees themselves represented an honorable line of men who were zealous in their observance and knowledge of the law. They were not the hypocrites and bigots of Christian propaganda. (2) We can expose a core story by removing the opening and closing verses (18:9 and 18:14), which Wilson regards as Lucan redactions. These verses function as a frame that recasts the core story as a parable of stiff-necked pride and humble repentance. The remaining core story itself goes back to an older version, perhaps to Jesus himself, which is both more radical and more revolutionary than Luke's polemic against the Pharisees. At the core of the older version is the insistence that there is no difference that makes a difference between these two men. In the older version the Pharisee is a good man who meets his obligations, does what is expected of him, gives to the poor, and avoids what is forbidden him, while the tax collector is indeed a collaborator and a sinner. But the point of the story is that God's gracious mercy is so bountiful that the difference between the men is leveled: the good deeds of the Pharisee hold no real weight before God, the sun of whose love and forgiveness rises upon both the good and the bad. Indeed, the sinful tax collector has a preferred access to God, while the Pharisee, having nothing to forgive, cannot "get in touch" with God.

On Wilson's more radical telling, the focus of the story shifts away from the Pharisee and the tax collector toward God. It is a parable about God as the giver of an unconditional or radical forgiveness, about God as the father of forgiveness. God forgives us without regard to our merits, thereby radically leveling the difference between the Pharisee, who does well, and the tax collector, who does not. God does not submit to the "conditions" under which forgiveness functions for human beings. Unlike human beings, God dispenses forgiveness unconditionally, not according to the conditions imposed by the principle of sufficient reason, the conditions we require to forgive one another.

Told in this way, the story of the Pharisee and the tax collector sounds a little like the parable of the prodigal son, which is also to be read as a parable not about the sons but about the father—let us say the prodigal father, who is himself, like God, prodigal with love and forgiveness. It is as if we could turn that famous line from Augustine's *Confessions* around and say that God has made us for himself and God cannot rest until he holds us in his embrace, for there is nothing we can do that he cannot forgive.

God is the God of gifts, of unconditional gifts, of giving and forgiving. Anselm said that God is that than which no greater can be conceived, that God's being is unconditioned, unrestricted by any conditions that would limit God to this finite and conceivable order or that. Just so, God's giving is that than which no greater can be conceived and, as such, is not conditioned by any conditions that would constrict God's giving under this or that finite constraint, this or that finite demand of reason. God is not constrained by the finite conditions of an economy of exchange, by the principle of reason. God's being and God's giving are "constrained" only by goodness and so marked by excess, by exceeding whatever finite constraints are imposed upon it by conceptual thinking.

The story, thus, is not about the vanity of the Pharisee or the humility of the tax collector, but about the surpassing greatness of God, which levels the difference between human achievements. In just the way God leveled the tower of Babel, he levels the difference between the moral heights and valleys of human achievement. Furthermore, beyond leveling the difference, the story even suggests a certain priority of the sinner, a certain perversion and inversion of the order of moral rank, in which sinners, who have more to be forgiven, get a larger share of the kingdom, and perhaps even priority seating.

Is not Wilson's rendering a scandal? Does not such a rendering suggest a moral anarchy, an "anything goes" relativism, a sacred anarchy or holy relativism, to be sure, in which God forgives all and makes the sun of forgiveness rise equally upon the good and the bad (Matt. 5:45), but a relativism just the same? Is it not a terrifying thought to anyone who thinks that we must be held responsible for what we do—and who does not?—and that whether we do well or do ill, justice on injustice, makes all the difference?

Wilson, however, is not a New Testament scholar and, as brilliantly suggestive as this page in his book is, he offers no evidence for his reading. Nor does he address the very real possibility that Luke has not misunderstood the story, but invented it himself. But Wilson's point is not without scholarly merit. One of the more unassailable things we know about Jesus, if there are any, is that forgiveness was a central part of his teachings. The historical Jesus was, as Hannah Arendt said, the master of forgiveness, and that may have played some role in the trouble that Jesus brought down on himself (Arendt 1958).

One has to be very careful in dealing with this matter, because it is very much steeped in Christian apologetics. The gift—the graciousness, the loving excess of God—tends to be the way Christians lay out the case for the superiority of the New Covenant over the Old. That is why I turn for guidance in these matters to E. P. Sanders, for he is a scholar who is acutely sensitive to Jesus' Jewish sources and to the excesses of Christian polemics. The Christian apologetes think, Sanders says, that "we [Christian New Testament scholars] have love, mercy, repentance, forgiveness, and even simple decency on our side, and that is why our religion is superior to its parent" (1985, 199).

As Derrida says, the scene of Christian apologetics is usually staged as a war against the Jews, in which the Christian is opposed to the Jew as honor is opposed to credit, the living word to the dead letter, the word of honor to the written contract, forgiveness and mercy to commerce, the love of the poor to the wealthy banker (Derrida 1992, 101 n. 18). In other words, and this is something that emerges from Derrida's *The Gift of Death*, Christianity defines itself in terms of love, grace, and the gift, while defining Judaism in terms of the eye-for-an-eye economy of legalism and externality.

With that in mind, let us follow Sanders's more scholarly and well-documented inquiry into the place of sinners in Jesus' preaching about the kingdom and just what was so disturbing about it. If Jesus had simply been repeating the classical doctrine of Teshuvah, if he had simply been elaborating the traditional conditions under which atonement may be attained, he would not have attracted any attention to himself. To have brought down so much trouble upon his head, he must have introduced an innovation on the classical teaching that caused a collision with the religious establishment of the day. In Sanders's view, the one distinctive thing that "we may be certain marked Jesus' teaching about the kingdom is that it would include the 'sinners,' " that the kingdom had in a special way to do with the lost sheep (1985, 174).

By "sinners" (*hamertoloi*), Sanders insists, we do not mean the righteous who have repented of their sin, but those who are still sinning, even "professional" sinners, those who earn their living by sin (such as usurers, tax collectors, prostitutes). By associating with them, Jesus earned a great deal of criticism for himself. The kingdom has to do with those who are "lost" (*apololos*): the lost sheep, the lost coin, the lost son (Lk. 15:4, 6, 9, 32). Even if we concede that the expression "there is more joy in heaven over one sinner who repents" is a bit of Luke's editorializing, still he is on the right track (Sanders 1985, 179).

The sinners, Sanders insists, are not to be confused with the "common people" (*amme ha-arets*). As Jesus would not have caused a stir by ministering to the righteous who sin no more, so he would not have caused a stir by ministering to the poor, to common and uneducated people, who were certainly not irreligious. To have fallen afoul of the powers that be, he must have mingled with and offered the kingdom to the wicked, to those who flagrantly disobeyed the law (Sanders 1985, 187).

The challenge Jesus posed did not lie in letting the common people into the kingdom, for they had not been excluded in the first place. The only ones who thought commoners were excluded were those who held the cynical view of the Pharisees cultivated in Christian polemics, in which these Jews were portrayed as a small purity group who excluded everyone but themselves from the kingdom. This, Sanders argues, has more to do with Christian polemics than historical research. The common people were un-educated, which may have diminished their responsibility about the fine points of the law, and they did not observe priestly purity laws, which would have been something they needed to remedy if and when they wanted to enter the temple. But neither of these things would make them wicked or "sinners."

What caused Jesus so much trouble, Sanders argues, is not that he was inclusive of the common, uneducated people, as opposed to the bigoted Pharisees who were exclusive of everybody but themselves. Although it is certainly true that Jesus was inclusive, that he was a "champion of plain folk" (1985, 198), no right-minded observer of the Jewish law would have objected to some-one ministering to the poor and uneducated. Rather, what must have brought so much trouble down upon Jesus was that he of-fered the kingdom to the wicked, to sinners who were still sin-ning.

Once again, caution is required. As Sanders points out, that sinners could be forgiven, that forgiveness was always available to those who had a change of heart, both on an individual basis and to Israel as a nation, is a standard part of Jewish theology and would have been well known to Jesus the Jew (Sanders 1985, 106–8). In Ezekiel's famous discourse on Teshuvah (33:10–20), the Lord God says, "I have no pleasure in the death of the wicked, but that the wicked turn from their ways and live; turn back, turn back from your evil ways . . . and as for the wickedness of the wicked, it will not make them stumble when they turn from their wickedness." If they turn from their sins, restore what they have stolen, and sin no more, "they shall surely live. None of the sins that they have committed shall be remembered against them." Teshuvah, which we tend to translate into English as "repen-tance," derives from the verb *to turn* or *return* (*shuv*): "Return, O Israel, to the Lord, your God, for you have stumbled because of your iniquity" (Hos. 14:1). This was translated in the LXX as *apos-trepho,* to turn away from, to turn back from, wickedness, which also links up with metanoia in the New Testament: to be trans-formed into and to take on a new mind. If Jesus taught a doctrine of the need for sinners to repent or "return," he would have just been saying something very Jewish, something already found in Ezekiel and Hosea, and that would hardly have attracted any unfavorable attention to him. Repentance was also the salient motif of the preaching of the Baptist, although, unlike the Baptist, who was concerned with national repentance, Jesus seems to have had individual transgressions in mind.

We ought not to imagine that the Pharisees were offended by love, mercy, and grace, by the graciousness of the forgiving God preached by Jesus while they themselves, being hard of heart, demanded punishment, an eye for an eye, a merciless retribution for every transgression. Indeed, the evangelists portray the Pharisees not only as not forgiving, but also as willing to kill anyone who taught forgiveness (Sanders 1985, 201–2). As Sanders says, the standard Christian renderings of the Jews make it difficult to understand how Jesus could have been a Jew himself and lived as a Jew, and they deprive Jesus of "a living context in Judaism" (1985, 18). In fact, as Sanders argues, repentance and forgiveness were staples of Jewish theology, and had Jesus been able to turn the tax collectors and thieves around, to effect a change of heart in them and bring them back into the fold, he would have been hailed as a national hero.

What then—if anything—was Jesus saying about forgiveness to give offense?

Might it have concerned the time of forgiveness? Might it have been that Jesus offered forgiveness to sinners who were still sinning, and this in advance of their having repented? Then the line that divided Jesus from his critics was this: traditional Judaism offered "conditional forgiveness," forgiveness only to those who had repented, who had become righteous; while Jesus offered what might be called "unconditional forgiveness," forgiveness in advance to those who were still sinning. On this telling, the Pharisees said, "God forgives you if you repent"; Jesus said, "God forgives you, so go repent and mend your ways." "The gift," Sanders says, "should precede the demand" (1985, 204). The gift of grace would precede repentance. That is a difference that makes a difference, but, however interesting and provocative a theological point it may be, it hardly seems likely that it would have caused much of an offense, or that Jesus would have been led to the cross by this distinction. On the whole, it seems the Jewish people would have been delighted if, after Jesus had dined with the usurers and tax collectors and told them that God forgave them, the usurers had been led to give up their usury, or the tax collectors to give up their collaboration with Rome. Such an offer of forgiveness, moreover, would hardly have been unconditional, for Jesus would have simply been offering them forgiveness "on credit." The timing would have been different—it would have been given in advance—but he would have expected follow-through; if he had been thinking like a banker, he would have expected them to keep up with the payments.

Sanders's own proposal is this: while the Jewish law required repentance and restitution—Ezekiel is very clear about this (33:15)—Jesus may have earned the wrath of the religious authorities of the day by offering forgiveness to sinners not only while they were still sinners, and not only in advance, on condition that they subsequently give up sinning, but rather without requiring restitution and repentance. That would also have sharpened the difference between Jesus and the Baptist, who most certainly required repentance and, as we have seen, on a national scale. It is not that Jesus did not desire that sinners repent, but that he did not insist on it, perhaps because John the Baptist was doing a good job of making the need for repentance clear, and because his own particular mission was to address the outsiders, the sinners who were still sinning (Sanders 1985, 227).

In the story of Levi the tax collector (Mk. 2:13–17; Lk. 5:27–32), there is no mention in any of its versions that the tax collector gave up his profession, but only that Jesus "called" him and he "followed." It may be that this means Jesus had among his followers tax collectors who remained tax collectors, which was what drew down the fire of the authorities upon him. If Jesus was saying that the kingdom was ours if we followed him, not if we repented and made restitution, that would have put him at odds not with hypocrites and bigots, but with Ezekiel, Hosea, and the mainstream faithful of Judaism.

When Levinas remarks in *Nine Talmudic Lectures* that "there is no forgiveness that has not been requested by the guilty," that is, by those who have had a change of heart, he is commenting on a passage of Mishnah that is a classical element in Jewish theology of forgiveness (Levinas 1999, 19). If, in addition, Jesus said that the sinners would get priority seating in the kingdom, that there was some kind of preferential priority not for the poor, but for

the wicked—if he did indeed say, "The tax collectors and prostitutes are going into the kingdom ahead of you" (Matt. 21:31),
that would have added fuel to the fires that eventually consumed
Jesus. That would have made Jesus' offer of unconditional forgiveness a little more unconditional, inasmuch as he would not have
withdrawn his offer if the sinner continued to sin.

That would indeed constitute a certain madness, as Derrida
would say: an act of forgiving that utterly jettisons the demand for
a reason for forgiveness. And it would redirect the focal point of
Jesus' teaching about forgiveness to the God of forgiveness and
away from the sinners themselves, or the difference between the
good and wicked. That would constitute a maddening madness,
which frustrates a certain need or impulse we all feel, to use the
strictly economic terms we employ on these occasions, to get
even, to even or settle the score, a point that would lead us back
to Nietzsche's *Genealogy of Morals*. For it is just maddening that
someone would get off scot-free, without having to pay for what
he did. It offends all economy, our economic reason, which cannot tolerate this sort of disequilibrium.

Jesus' views on sinners and repentance invite a comparison with
the command given to the young man who wanted to follow him
but who wanted first to bury his father. When Jesus told the young
man to follow him at once and unconditionally, and to let the
dead bury the dead (Matt. 8:21f, Luke 9:59–60), he was suspend-
ing a precept that was sacred in both the Jewish and Greco-Roman
worlds (that, of course, is just about what Creon told Antigone).
Jesus thereby indicated, if not outright opposition to the law (as a
good many New Testament scholars think), at least the willingness
to claim that the law was not enough, not the last word, not final
(Sanders 1985, 267), and this not because he opposed it, but because he thought humanity was in transition to the coming of a
new age, of the kingdom.

Thus, if one followed him and heeded his call about the coming of the kingdom, then certain provisions of the law—such as
burying the dead and doing repentance—might, on occasion, be
suspended or superseded (Sanders 1985, 255). That sort of thing,
which "challenged the adequacy of the law," would have attracted
the attention of the priests, who "were the administrators of the

law, and also those who were authorized to say whether or not atonement had been made or purity achieved" (1985, 300).

That, Sanders argues, casts the Christian-Jewish polemic in a clearer light. This was not a debate between the lovers of the gift and cold-hearted legalists. There was no disagreement between Jesus and his contemporaries, his fellow Jews, about whether God was loving, gracious, and forgiving. Everyone was agreed on the beauty and the value of the "gift," so long as it was taken abstractly. What they disagreed about was whether the gift of forgiving occurred under the concrete conditions of repentance and restitution traditionally required by the law and set forth explicitly in Ezekiel, or whether God granted forgiveness unconditionally, without repentance and restitution, to those who followed Jesus.

Jesus was being opposed not by bigots and hypocrites, the unworthy opponents whom Matthew devised (Matt. 23)—and this is the text that Derrida seizes upon in *The Gift of Death*—but by earnest and responsible religious people who were offended by his views on forgiveness. They were also offended by the importance he attached to himself and to those disciples who followed him, from whom the demands of the law could, on occasion, be lifted, and by his claim to be God's spokesman and to know what God was going to do next (Sanders 1985, 280, 293). But all these things were theological fine points compared with Jesus' attack on the temple and his prediction of its fall, which, in Sanders's view, was the main thing that led him to the cross (1985, 300).

There is another dimension to the question of the time of forgiveness. It may be, Sanders notes, that Jesus desired the repentance of the sinners, but did not demand it because he thought the sinners did not have the time to remake their lives (1985, 207–8). It may be that he was convinced that the end time was at hand, and that at this eschatological moment, sinners would not be given the time required for the lifelong work of making themselves into new beings and making restitution, undoing the damage they had caused. In the urgent moment of the end time, God issued a blanket amnesty. If, however, Jesus' notion of forgiveness was forged under the peculiar circumstance of the end time, that would mean that it was not absolutely unconditional, but subject to the peculiar condition that the end was at hand. It may have been a peculiarly eschatological notion, where there was time for metanoia only if that meant to be of a new mind, but no time for metanoia if that meant the more elaborate work of restitution and striking out on a new course in life.

If one thinks that time is up, then the future takes on a rather different sense and cannot become a necessary condition. Forgiveness, like justice, cannot wait. Like justice, forgiveness deferred would be forgiveness denied. Forgiveness cannot depend upon the future reform of one's life if there is no future. Forgiveness cannot depend upon sinning no more, if there is no "more." If one thinks the end is at hand, time is over, then everything is changed.

That puts the church that survived Jesus in a tough spot. For when the end time did not come about and the church began, as it were, to unpack its bags and to prepare for a longer stay, it faced a difficult decision: whether to stay with this radical teaching of unconditional forgiveness, or to reinstate the traditional conditions. The gospels of the latter half of the first century leave no doubt about the course that the church followed. The choice to get back in line with the mainstream tradition is plainly in evidence throughout the gospel of Luke, in his insistence on the conditions, on the need for repentance and sinning no more.

That would also explain why Luke was motivated to give us a revised version of a pre-Lucan story about a Pharisee and a tax collector in the way that A. N. Wilson suggests, if that indeed is what happened. It is impossible to tell if that is what Jesus had in mind. Would he have settled for the more traditional doctrine if he concluded that he had been jumping the gun about the end time? Was his offer of unconditional forgiveness subject to the eschatological condition, so that Jesus too would have required a follow-up repentance and restitution if he had come to see that there was, indeed, time enough to undertake it?

Or was the forgiveness of which he spoke indeed unconditional, absolutely unconditional, that is, offered to someone without regard to repentance, as a pure gift, because the unrepentant sinner who was still sinning was the one who most needed forgiveness, the repentant having already put their lives back in order? Unconditional forgiveness would have constituted the greater paradox and the greater scandal, which, on the criteria set forth by Johannes Climacus, would have required the greater passion, intensity, and faith—all of which are marks of greater subjective truth, of an objective uncertainty held fast in passionate inwardness. But even on the criteria set forth by Sanders, that he must have taught something that had a particularly scandalous force to have been brought to the cross by it, the notion of an absolutely unconditional forgiveness seems a more likely hypothesis. That, in turn, would lend some support to the radical reading of the story of the Pharisee and tax collector who went up to the temple to pray.

Forgetting the Past: It Never Happened

"None of the sins that they have committed shall be remembered against them," Ezekeiel says in his famous hymn to repentance (Ez. 33:16). "For I will forgive their iniquity, and remember their sin no more," says the Lord in Jeremiah (31:37). Derrida, in *Given Time*, and in evident agreement with the prophets (whom he does not cite), tells us that the gift requires absolute forgetting. The one who is offended must forget the offense, even as the offender must be able to put the offense behind him and move on, beyond the offense but also beyond the forgiveness, lest he incur a life-long debt. The offended must forget the offense even as the offender must forget the forgiveness. Forgiveness requires absolute forgetting: the trespass is over, I dismiss what you have done to me, we should both forget it.

Indeed, when we give the gift of forgiveness, one of the things we say to the debtor or trespasser is, "Forget it. It never happened." The time of the gift on this account is most amazing, for it requires a past that ceases to be: in forgiveness, it is to be as if it never happened. Forgiven time is not to be confused with a revisionist history, in which a propaganda machine wipes out our knowledge of the past. Forgiveness would, if it could, strike a blow against the past itself. The past would be wiped out, annulled or erased, so that, were it possible, it really would be the case that it never happened.

The longing for such an undoable past was the beautiful dream of the medieval theologian St. Peter Damian (1005–72), who signed his work *Petrus peccator monachus,* "Peter, monk and sinner." Peter entertained a low opinion of philosophers—he is reputed to have said that if philosophy had been necessary, Jesus would have chosen philosophers for his disciples instead of fishermen with the jawbone of an ass! Peter maintained the primacy of the good over being, of goodness of God over whatever is, so that God could do whatever it was good to do, and Peter was outraged at the dialecticians who thought their anemic academic arguments could curtail the almighty power of God. He thought them not worthy of a reply, contemptible, and he recommended branding them (Wippel and Wolter 1969, 147).[1] He thought it particularly insolent to deny, as did the dialecticians, that it belonged to the divine omnipotence to be able to undo what had been done in the past.

Thus God had the power to make it be that Rome had not been founded, even after it had been founded, and to make it be that what had been destroyed had not been destroyed—for example, to restore virginity *post ruinam,* as Peter said, after one had "lost it," as we say today. The argument Peter offered was this: If it once belonged to the power of God to do something or to prevent something from happening in the past, then, since God was eternal and unchanging and could not suffer from some limitation in the present that he had not been subject to in the past, then it still belonged to his power to see to it that this same thing would not have happened, even if it had happened. Peter wrote:

> For the same potency that he then possessed has neither changed nor been removed, but just as he always is what he is, so also God's potency cannot be changed. . . . Therefore, since God is always one and the same, so in him the power to do all things is always present, is unfailing and cannot pass away. . . . If, therefore, in every instance God is always able to do whatever he could do from the beginning, if he was able before the creation of things to cause whatever now

---

[1] See also Peter Damian, "De divina omnipotentia in reparatione Corruptae and factis Infectis Reddendis," in J. P. Migne, ed., *Patrologia Latina* (Paris, 1867), vol. 145, *Opuscula 36.* For a partial translation, see "On Divine Omnipotence," in Wippel and Wolter *1969,* 140–52. For commentaries, see Irven Michael Resnick, *Divine Power and Possibility in St. Peter Damian's De Divina Omnipotentia, Studien und Texte Zur Geistesgeschichte Des Mittelalters,* vol. 31 (Dordrecht: Brill Academic Publishers, 1992); and Irven Michael Resnick, "Repentance, Forgiveness, and God's Power over the Past: A Study of St. Peter Damian's *De divina omnipotentia*" (Charlottesville: University of Virginia Ph.D. thesis, 1983).

exists not to have existed in any way, he has the power, consequently, that the things that were made would not have been made
at all. Indeed his potency is fixed and eternal, so that whatever he
could have done at any moment he always has the power to do,
nor does the diversity of times suggest the presence of the slightest
change in eternity (Wippel and Wolter 1969, 149).

We must distinguish, Peter Damian insists, between the timeless
"can" (*potest*) in God's eternal present and the time-bound
"could have" (*potuit*) employed in human speech. When we say
that God could have seen to it that Rome would not have been
founded, that remains a "can be" or "can do" in the power of
God, whose present does not turn into a past. "Whatever God
could do, he doubtless also is able to do" (Wippel and Wolter
1969, 148).

Now, since God can do whatever it is good to do—here is the
pertinence of all this for our discussion of forgiveness—God has
the power to make it be that the forgiven sinner did not sin. By
distinguishing God's eternal point of view from our temporal
one, Damian is also, in effect, distinguishing two different points
of view with respect to time. From our point of view, which is
that of beings of finite power and fully submerged in the flow of
temporal consciousness, the past is irremissible, and this because
we have no power of disposition over it. From our point of view,
let us say, from a phenomenological point of view (which is, let
us not forget, the point of view of those who risk branding), Husserl got it right. The present flows off into the past, where it assumes a fixed and inalterable place. Something happened,
whether or not we know what happened, and that is the end of it.
There is nothing contingent here, no "could have happened,"
except as regards our limited knowledge.

But from God's point of view, where there is nothing finite, be
it spatial or temporal, that can resist his power, and where his
power does not ebb and flow but remains inalterably the same,
the past does not have irremissibility. If God could prevent something from happening now, then, since it is always now for God
and every moment of time is present to him, including past moments, God can always and already see to it that it does not happen, even if, from our point of view, it already did.

The hypothesis is remarkable in many respects. It is exactly the opposite of Nietzsche's hypothesis of eternal recurrence. Rather than assuming that what has happened in the past has indeed happened an infinite amount of times, we are not sure that what has happened in the past ever happened at all, even once. What we know of the past may or may not be what happened. Furthermore, what we remember now of the past, what we say happened in the past, may be the past that God has made to be by undoing what was done—and so the past, evil as it seems to us, may be filled with, or rather may have been emptied of, evils that God has undone.

Such untrammeled divine freedom set loose in the service of the divine goodness would give God disposition over the "laws" of morality—for nothing created can offer God's power resistance—which is the rather grumpy and Thomistic complaint of Frederick Copleston in the paragraph he gives Damian in his *History*. Damian, Copleston complains, betrays a certain sympathy with the interpretation of the contingent status of ethical laws offered by Johannes de Silentio in *Fear and Trembling* (Copleston 1966, 145–46).

Now, apart from the fact that this association with Johannes de Silentio does not represent for me, as it does for Fr. Copleston, a case of guilt by association, it is important to keep in mind Peter Damian's focus on divine goodness: that were God to suspend the laws of morality, it would be in the name of goodness. In my view, this would mean that God would suspend the universal in the name of the particular, that he would suspend the law in the name of justice, whenever it was good to do so. In this particularly amazing case of amazing grace that Damian has proposed, what was true then—that the sinner sinned—is not true now, not because the sinner has now ceased sinning or because the sinner is offered forgiveness in advance on condition that he cease sinning later, but because it is no longer true that the sinner sinned, the almighty power and bountiful goodness of God having seen to that.

Damian is usually taken to be violating the principle of noncontradiction, that is, to be defending the view that both p ("Rome was founded") and ~p ("It is not the case that Rome was founded") are, or could be, simultaneously true. But it has been nicely argued that he can be construed to be saying something else, that is, that there are no past facts, that the past has a radical contingency that mirrors the contingency of the future (Mc-Arthur and Slattery 1974, 137–41). Damian's argument, then, would be that we cannot make assertoric claims about the past—for example, either that Rome was or was not founded—but only modal claims, for example, that Rome might or might not have been founded, depending upon what God wants to be the case, which is very disconcerting but not contradictory.

In *de Interpretatione* 9, Aristotle wonders whether the contingent events of time do not tend to slide into necessity. For if it is true that something, say a sea fight, happened yesterday, is happening today, or will happen tomorrow, then it is necessarily true that it did happen, is happening, or will happen. That seems especially true as regards the past. Does not the past, the sphere of everything that was the case, acquire an inalterable necessity in virtue of its having happened, so that once it happened that there was a sea battle, it is always and necessarily true that there was such a sea battle?

That, in fact, is what the Stoics, or any determinist, hold. They agree with Damian that statements about the past are not assertoric, not because they take such statements to be contingent, but because they regard them as necessary. Damian holds the opposite view: that, far from acquiring necessity, the past remains every bit as contingent after it happens as before it happens.

That is because Damian was a monk and a sinner—that is, a Christian with a biblical frame of mind, a theologian who believed in the power of God to make all things new, who believed that time no less than space offered no real resistance to God (who made them both), and that philosophers who offered resistance to theology should have been taken out and branded. He thus consented with enthusiasm to the idea of the changeover from nonbeing to being that we call creation, as regards physical things, and grace and metanoia as regards spiritual things, which also can be seen as a changeover from being to nonbeing, when that is what the divine goodness thinks is best.

Damian believed in the gift, the expenditure without return, while the Greeks were wary of those who bore such a gift. Because for Damian nothing could resist the mighty power of God, including time itself, time acquired an astonishing contingency. Beyond the contingency of the future (which seems easy to swallow), or

of the present (which sometimes seems contingent and sometimes like a bind), Damian, God bless him, affirmed the contingency of the past. *Mirabile dictu!* Amazing grace! The density of
time was hollowed out for Damian by the omnipotence of God.

The Greeks, on the other hand, who simply did not spend
enough time reading the Jewish scriptures and who, alas, came
too soon for the Christian ones, had an altogether different idea
of time and God. For Damian, the meaning of God was untrammeled goodness, power and freedom, which introduced an astonishing contingency into things, while for the Greeks, the very idea
of the divine meant the unchanging and immortal, and so the
divine tended to introduce a considerable necessity, an immobil-
ity into things.

The Greeks divided everything up into unchanging being and
changing being, immortals up above and mortals down below,
and they prized above all the things that could not be otherwise,
about which they said there was alone true episteme. So the effect
of their love of things divine was to prize the necessary, immobile,
and universal over the contingent, changing, and singular. They
constantly sought to see to it that mortal and changing things
strove after and sought to be as unchanging as their humble circumstances permitted, instead of seeing that the infinite elasticity
and contingency of time was a manifestation of the omnipotence
of God.

The Greeks were scandalized by the idea that being would
come from nonbeing, that something could be made from nothing, that any transition could be made between being and nonbeing, and they assigned a great deal more prestige to what was
unchanging about the changing world around them than to
change itself. They wanted to fit the things that changed into a
schema where the unchanging had the primacy, to subordinate
the changing things that just happened to a thing (*symbebekos*) to
what that thing permanently was (*ousia*), and, in general, to insert
contingent things into schemata where necessity ruled. So when
they looked upon the heavenly bodies, which they regarded as the
most unchanging of material bodies, they sought to have them
move in circles, which contained their endless motion within an
unchanging pattern.

That, of course, is exactly the line of argument advanced against

the Greeks by Johannes Climacus in *Philosophical Fragments* and by
Constantine Constantius in *Repetition*. The Greeks, Constantius
said, had their doubts about movement and kinesis and, beginning with the Eleatics, tended to deny it ultimate status either by
denying it outright, as in Parmenides, or by making it a copy of
something unchanging, as in Plato, or by assigning it a real but
subordinate status in the ousiological order, as in Aristotle.

So if there must be motion, as indeed there must, it would be
better to go around in a circle, a cyclical motion offering us
the best imitation of eternity (and that is the motion of the otherwise immutable heavenly bodies), or else to go backward, which
is the motion of anamnesis, which treats the movement from ig-
norance into knowledge as the recollection of what has already
taken place. But in the religions of the Book, as Constantine Constantius said, we prefer not to move in circles or go backward, but
to press forward into new territory, to go where we have not been
before, to let something new happen. In the more biblical point
of view advanced by Constantine Constantius and Johannes Climacus, we prize the most what the Greeks would never allow, what
they will not permit us to either say or think, which is that there
could be a movement from nonbeing to being. As regards the
world itself, such a movement is what the religions of the Book
call creation. As regards human freedom, it is the capacity to
make a radical change of course, from one direction to another.
Beyond freedom, as regards grace, it is the power of God to give
us a second gift, the gift of a new birth or new heart, metanoia, to
turn us around (Teshuvah).

That is also why, for the believers in the religions of the Book,
Constantine said that eternity is always up ahead, in the *vita ven-
tura,* the life to come, *l'avenir, l'à-venir,* something to be achieved
by freedom, by pressing forth in a forward repetition, by putting
our hands to the plow and not looking back. In the religions of
the Book the rallying cry is always, to borrow a phrase from Augustinus Franco-Judaeus, *viens, oui, oui.*

That is why forgiveness, which requires much humility, is so
central in the biblical scheme. Forgiveness is an impossible attempt to do something impossible—to say "it never happened."
Even and especially if it did. Forgiveness is a sign of our love of
the impossible. Forgiveness is a blow struck by the good at being

and the past, a *reductio ad nihilum,* which reduces the being of an offense to nonbeing, which wipes it out without a trace, which has the effect of recreating the offender, effecting a new life in the offender by leading the offender from nonbeing into being, into metanoia.

I should say—at the risk of being branded—that I am recommending that we read Damian's treatise on the divine omnipotence less as a metaphysical argument than as a bit of saintly excess, as a hyperbolic theory of forgiveness that can, for example, help us understand the radical reading of the story of the tax collector and the Pharisee proposed by A. N. Wilson.[2] On this reading, the tax collector has indeed sinned but has been forgiven by the bountiful mercy of God. His sin has been wiped away, so that he now enjoys equal status with the Pharisee. He has been made new and is of a new mind and new heart, metanoia; he has turned around, Teshuvah. Thanks be to the God of mercy who says to the tax collector, forget it, it never happened. There has been a radical leveling of the difference between the Pharisee and the tax collector. Inasmuch as they are both turned toward God, they are both pure and thank God for lifting them up, and hence they are both Pharisees. But insofar as even the Pharisee too has sometimes fallen, they have both been forgiven, and hence they are both tax collectors asking God for his mercy. Are we not all Pharisees and tax collectors, and do we not show both sides, and is there not a holy undecidability between them?

One last point: have we not said that the peculiar scandal offered by Jesus lies in consorting with sinners who are still sinning, not those who have repented of their sins and been forgiven, but those who, like the tax collectors, earn a living by their sin, who have sinned in the past and whose sins, far from having ceased, still persist? To be sure. But we must, following Damian, distinguish God's point of view and ours. Jesus invites us to see the

---

[2] I hold, God help me, at the risk of branding: If by divine omnipotence we mean that God can do anything, then to see to it that something was both done and not done, made and not made, is not a "thing," not a possible, but what the medievals called a *flatus vocis.* One's lips are moving but nothing is getting said. It would no more limit God's omnipotence to say that God "cannot" make something have happened and not have happened than it would to say that God "cannot" do evil, since even Damian admits that God is "constrained" by the good. What Damian says is long on praise, short on predication.

sinner from God's point of view, from the point of view of the kingdom, where there is an absolute remissibility of sin, for it is only God who can forgive sin, and that is the point of view from which Damian wants to see things. But from the human point of view, which is also the point of view of the sinner, sin has a recurrent and irremissible quality, for we sin again and again and our guilt seems irremissible. That is why Jesus both preaches about the forgiveness of sins and consorts with sinners. From the point of view of the kingdom, the sinner who has sinned, who sins again, has had his sin lifted by God as many times as he sins, even if he sins seven times a day, or seven times seven. In the kingdom, there is no sin that overtakes the divine omnipotence, no sin that God could not wipe away. For the kingdom is where God rules, where nothing can resist his rule.

Never Forget: The Time of Confession

Up to now, we have approached the gift of forgiveness from the standpoint of one who is offended, the one who must give this gift (for we cannot give it to ourselves), and we have identified the time of forgiving as one of absolute forgetting. Let us now consider the standpoint of the offender, where time takes the very different form of a work of memory. Let us approach this question by following a valuable discussion in Rosenzweig and Levinas, recently brought to our attention by Robert Gibbs.[3] What tense is the sinner—Rozenzweig is speaking of sin—to use to describe his state? Should he say:

> I am a sinner?
> I was a sinner?
> I have been a sinner?

We know that in Alcoholics Anonymous, experience teaches us that members should begin by giving their name and confessing "I am an alcoholic," and this on the well-founded belief that if they say their alcoholism is behind them, they will fail to see it

---

[3] The following discussion is greatly indebted to the analysis of forgiveness in Robert Gibbs's *Why Ethics? Signs of Responsibilities* (2000, chaps. 14–16). See pages 307–53, especially 334–37.

lying in wait for them up ahead. According to Rosenzweig, however, the first word we hear from the sinner is "I have been a
sinner"—up to now, but now it is over, past and gone. I have put
it behind me and made it go away (Rosenzweig 1971, 180).

At this moment, "the I that speaks is not the sinning one"
(Gibbs 2000, 334) But that initial confession, according to Rosenzweig, is to be followed by a second, more encompassing confession: "I am a sinner" (Rosenzweig 1971, 180). Even with these
other sins behind me, I have not become a pure will. I continue
to fall, and I have no illusions about my weakness and imperfec-
tion. After all, even Peter Damian, who was extremely optimistic
about our ability to heal the past, signed his name "monk and
sinner," as if the two went naturally together, as if he was a monk
just because he was a sinner.

From the standpoint of the gift, which always involves an excess
beyond economy, we might say that in confessing "I am still and
will ever be a sinner," I am aiming at the excess of unconditional
responsibility. In a discussion of marriage in *Either/Or*, the author
of the letters of "B" tells us that in a marriage that has been
reduced to an economy—we will use Derrida's language—each
partner will seek to justify his or her actions before the other, to
prove that he or she is in the right. But in a marriage built on
love—that is, the gift—the two partners will eagerly seek to put
themselves in the wrong for the sake of the love, each attempting
to assume all blame and all responsibility—without a calculation,
without an objective adjudication of who is right and who is
wrong, the very thought of such a calculation representing a kind
of violation of the love. Each will compete with the other in a
kind of potlatch of confession, each seeking to outdo the other
in assuming blame, each seeking to assume all the responsibility
and to leave the other blameless so that the love may flourish.
Love says, "It is all my fault, all my doing," whereas the law weighs
both sides according to the principle of sufficient reason.

Hence, in just the way we speak of the surpassing generosity of
a God who forgives unconditionally, we can in a parallel way speak
of the surpassing responsibility of the offender. If God's excess
is one of unconditional generosity, the sinner's excess is one of
unconditional responsibility. What moves us most about the tax
collector is that he puts up no defense. He stands far off, not even

looking up to heaven, but beating his breast and saying, "God be merciful to me, a sinner."

He stands far off and does not make a display of himself. He approaches God with bowed head and without a word in his own defense. He does not say that on the whole, taking into account that he has done a lot of good things in his life, he is on balance a sinner, or that he has been having a particularly bad time of late—he has lost his job and his wife is ill—and that is why he is a sinner, or that while it is true that he is a bit of a sinner, still every bloke deserves a break once in a while. He just lays down every defense in advance. His gift is to give up every defense that would excuse his conduct.

Even if there were a defense to be made, it is for God, or for the other, to make it on my behalf. Putting up a defense is not the business of the sinner, but of the one who has been sinned against. The sinner holds himself irrecusably responsible, makes himself wholly responsible, without availing himself of excuse or exoneration. Indeed, the onus is lifted if and only if I do not exonerate myself. That is why, in addition to saying that this sin is behind me, I then confess that I am and continue to be a sinner. In that moment, the time of forgiveness is given.

Forgiveness must come from the other. The sinner does not allow himself even to entertain the thought that he can unilaterally undo what he has done, unilaterally balance the accounts. He gives up, gives away any possible claim that he can in any way earn or deserve forgiveness. The sinner will always remember a certain unforgivability in the offense, so that if the one who is offended, in the idealized magnanimity of forgiveness, urges the sinner to "forget it, it was (it must become) nothing," then, for the idealized sorrow of the offender, it was everything and, therefore, quite unforgettable.

From the perspective of the sinner, the past is to be conserved, not lost, lest it revisit him in the future, so that the offender's duty is to remember the harm done to the other. So if, from the point of view of the giver of forgiveness, the temporality of forgiveness lies in "forget it, it never happened," then from the point of view of the sinner, the one who gives not a gift but an offense, the temporality of forgiveness lies in the "never forget."

But does this mean that we are to be held forever prisoners of the past, that the weight of the past is never to be lifted? Do the two temporalities—forget it/never forget, it was nothing/it is everything—simply contradict each other, the one annulling the other? Does forgiveness prove to be impossible because it rests upon a simple contradiction?

For relief from this dilemma let us turn to Levinas, who distinguishes the deed from the memory of the deed. The past is inalterable as a rock, not only metaphysically or logically, pace Peter Damian, but phenomenologically, because of its singularity. A lost child can never be replaced even though parents may have another child; the memories, the family keepsakes, the photographs, the aromas of a home destroyed by fire can never be replaced, even though a house with the same market value can be constructed in its place; the grief caused by disloyalty to a friend in the past lasts a lifetime even though one may never be disloyal again.

Still, Levinas says, we can "give the past a new meaning," repair the past by retelling the story of the past in a new narrative in which the past is given a new perspective, which frees or opens up the future (Levinas 1961, 259–60; 282–83). In this text Levinas has in mind what he calls "the discontinuous time of absolute youth," that is, the discretely different existence of the parent and the child, in which the child represents a new beginning, a separate life that does not bear the sins of the parent.

But the discontinuity of time can be applied as well to the lifetime of a single individual. If I am forgiven, I am given a new life. The rush of the past into the present is interrupted, and I am sufficiently separated from the past as to be allowed to breathe again. Forgiveness effects a kind of sacred discontinuity with myself. As Levinas says: "This recommencement of the instant, this triumph of the time of fecundity over the mortal and aging being's becoming, is a forgiveness, the very work of time" (1961, 282).

Husserlian time proves to be inadequate as regards both forgiveness and confession: the irremissible retention of the past is an obstacle to forgiving, where the deed should be forgotten; and the continuous flow of the present into the past proves to be an obstacle to being forgiven, where it is discontinuity. A breach with the past is required. Levinas, like Kierkegaard—both biblical thinkers—thinks of time along Cartesian lines, treating each moment as a new creation, which allows the past to lapse and life to begin anew. The time of forgiving is the giving of a new time, a gift of time, of a new beginning, a second chance. Forgiveness is a giving of time. *Pardonner: donner le temps.*

We are, thus, drawn back to the paradox first explored by Peter Damian, of the reversibility of time, of an action with a retroactive effect, that reaches back into the past and alters it. But unlike his medieval antecedent, Levinas gives this reversibility a purely ethical rather than a metaphysical sense. Peter Damian was so filled with confidence in the bountiful power and goodness of God, so sure that goodness was beyond being, that he confronted the metaphysicians and their metaphysics of presence head-on. He said that there was nothing on heaven or earth, in space or in time, neither present nor past, that could resist the mighty sway of God's love, and if being or presence or the principle of contradiction stood in God's way, then so much the worse for being or presence or the principle of contradiction. Levinas would think that Damian's hyperbolic heart was in the right place, that he rightly loved the good beyond being. But he does not share Damian's appetite for speculative argumentation. (It is of no little interest to note, however, that in Damian the effect of his philosophical argument is hardly to submit God to the philosophical procrustean bed of what Levinas calls "ontology." On the contrary, Damian is ready to cut off the feet of the philosophers, whom he seems also ready to roast alive, in order to meet the needs of the divine omnipotence.)

Still, I think that Levinas would hold that what Damian was getting at should be approached in rigorously ethical terms. Forgiveness reverses the past not because it changes it "physically," as it were, but because it alters its significance, gives it a new meaning and thereby repairs the past. Forgiveness does not alter the past itself, as in Damian, but the meaning of the past. As for the past itself, that is not altered but conserved and given a new sense; it undergoes a change of sign, as Husserl might say, into the mode of the "as if." It is henceforth as if it had never happened.

Hence, for the sinner the past is not forgotten, which would simply annul his relation with the past and destroy his responsibility; nor is it distorted and manipulated, which is what happens in revisionist history, which is always written by the oppressor; nor is it undone, as in Damian, which is a beautiful thought for the one who gives forgiveness unconditionally, but it does not quite do for one who has given up every defense and assumed unconditional responsibility. Rather, the past is conserved and "cleansed," which means reinterpreted.

On Damian's account, the sinner would no longer be guilty, would no longer actually have done the deed, would have been made innocent of the deed, so that the deed itself would have been washed away. On Levinas's account, the sinner has been forgiven but has not thereby become innocent; the deed has been cleansed, but not washed away. Beyond merely redescribing the past, but short of physically undoing it, forgiveness "cleanses the event" by "repeating" the past as forgiven. While the past is not actually altered, forgiveness permits the sinner "to be as if that instant had not elapsed, to be as if the subject had not committed himself" (Levinas 1961, 283).

What Damian would permit in an unqualified sense as part of the unlimited power of God, Levinas casts in the mode of the as if, marked by a new sign. But, as Gibbs points out, the power to alter the past is not invested in the sinner but in the one who is sinned against: "It is forgiveness that changes the past, *not* repentance" (2000, 351).

Now since, as Levinas argues in *Time and the Other,* time is not my doing, not the achievement of the running of the clock of internal time consciousness, but the accomplishment in me of the other who represents an absolutely unforeseeable future, then the gift of forgiveness from the other belongs to the way the other, in forgiving me, gives me time. By releasing me from my past, the other gives me a new past and, hence, a new future.

Surprisingly, Levinas even grants a certain "distinction" or eminence to the sinner, a certain superiority of being forgiven over having remained innocent all along. The surprise, of course, is that this reminds us of Jesus' sayings in the New Testament: that there is more joy in heaven over the lost sheep who is found than over the ones who never strayed. Indeed, Levinas attributes a "surplus of happiness" to the forgiven fall, which he describes as a *felix culpa,* citing the Christian Latin expression in the Easter vigil liturgy that refers to the happy fault of Adam's fall that was worthy to have such and so great a Redeemer.[4] *O felix culpa, quae talem et tantum meruit habere Redemptorem.* The human race is better off post ruinam, having sinned and been redeemed and thus lifted up by the supernatural grace brought by Christ, than it would have been in remaining all along in the state of nature, *integritas naturae,* in which case Christ's coming would have not have been precipitated.[5]

"O truly necessary sin of Adam," the liturgy says, "that is wiped out by the death of Christ" (*O certe necessarium Adae peccatum, quod Christi morte deletum est*).[6] Levinas does not shrink from using this central Christian narrative as a model for forgiveness, in virtue of which there is a higher grace in the forgiven misdeed than in steady loyalty to the law, even as a scarred tissue is stronger than the unwounded flesh, even as a converted sinner can, like Augustine, become a passionate saint.[7]

THE PHARISEE AND THE TAX COLLECTOR REVISITED

Let us now revisit this story one last time. Two men go up to the temple and stand before God, one, by any human reckoning, an honorable man who honors the law, who could, if anyone could, stand the scrutiny of good and evil; the other, by anyone's reckoning, a sinner. But by going up to the temple, they stand before God, the giver of all good gifts, and not before the bar of the law.

---

[4] This passage from Levinas (1961, 284) is insightfully commented on by Gibbs (2000, 351–53).

[5] To be sure, by pointing out that in virtue of the *felix culpa,* it will have been better sometimes to conserve the sin rather than to undo it, lest we prevent in advance the saintly convert or the advent of Jesus himself, we would not necessarily be contradicting Peter Damian. Peter would agree that when that is indeed what is better, then that is precisely what God would do, because God, who is constrained only by goodness, not being, always does what it is better to do. But when that is not better, there is nothing about being, past or present, that can block his power.

[6] F. X. Lasance and Francis Walsh, *The New Roman Missal in Latin and English* (New York: Benziger Brothers, 1956), 494.

[7] See Gibbs (2000), *Why Ethics?* chap. 17, for an excellent discussion of the social construction of time, and the need for a community to repent and be forgiven, to forget and remember. This is an extension of the topic that I cannot undertake here.

They have gone up to stand before the gift where there is no giving and taking of reasons, no *ratio reddenda,* no weighing of comparative merits and demerits. In the kingdom of the gift, every human measure, every economy, is suspended. Here the only rule is God's rule, which is the rule of justice, not the law, which means the rule of the gift.

Before the court of reason, there is all the difference in the world between these two men. But before God, who makes the sun of his love rise upon the righteous and the sinner, the distance between them is leveled, for he loves the son who has been loyal to him all the days of his life even as he rejoices in the son who has come home. The Pharisee gives God praise for the sins he has escaped, not by his own resources but by the bottomless grace of God; while the tax collector, who gives up every defense of his past, casts himself upon God's bountiful mercy.

Now allow me, in a final, farcical twist, to insert two more figures into this famous evangelical scene. The first, Peter Damian, *monachus peccator,* takes notes in Latin on what unfolds before him. He speculates on just what God could do to heal this tax collector if he took it into his divine mind and divine omnipotence to do something for the man. The second, Augustinus Judaeus, the author of *Circonfessions,* in a dark, distant corner of the temple, takes notes in Christian Latin French and is struck by the undecidability of the scene, by the strange logic that effects a confluence and reversibility of the tax collector and the Pharisee. He marvels at the remarkable effects of the gift in this scene, which depicts a time of giving and forgiving.

BIBLIOGRAPHY

Arendt, Hannah. 1958. *The Human Condition.* Chicago: University of Chicago Press.

Copleston, Frederick. 1966. *A History of Philosophy.* Vol. 2, *Augustine to Scotus.* London: Burns and Oates.

Derrida, Jacques. 1992. *Given Time.* Trans. P. Kamuf. Chicago: University of Chicago Press.

Gibbs, Robert. 2000. *Why Ethics? Signs of Responsibilities.* Princeton: Princeton University Press.

Levinas, E. 1999. *Nine Talmudic Lectures*. Pittsburgh: Duquesne University Press.

———. 1961. *Totality and Infinity*. Pittsburgh: Duquesne University Press.

McArthur, Robert P., and Michael P. Slattery. 1974. "Peter Damian and Undoing the Past," in *Philosophical Studies* 25: 137–41.

Rosenzweig, Franz. 1971. *The Star of Redemption*. Boston: Beacon.

Sanders, E. P. 1985. *Jesus and Judaism*. Philadelphia: Fortress Press.

Wilson, A. N. 1992. *Jesus: A Life*. New York: Fawcett Columbine.

Wippel, John F., and Allan B. Wolter, eds. 1969. *Medieval Philosophy: From St. Augustine to Nicholas of Cusa*. New York: Free Press.

7

Seneca against Derrida: Gift and Alterity

Jean-Joseph Goux

STOICISM IS the doctrine of antiquity that most vigorously and most radically opposes itself to every justification of action in terms of usefulness, interest, and profit. An action is good, virtuous in itself, regardless of any consideration of advantage or disadvantage, of pleasure or of pain felt by the one who does such an action. It must be accomplished because it has to be so, and not because the one who accomplishes it calculates or anticipates any benefit from such action.

And yet the Stoics, rigorously opposing themselves to any moral that considers profit as the goal of action, employ notions and vocabulary linked to the language of economics. Payment, salary, price, income, interest, trade, accountancy, debt, debit, and so on . . . this vocabulary is constantly put to work in the discourse of the Latin Stoics. It is both from and against these notions that Stoicism attempts to safeguard a modality of action—the relations between oneself and the others, divinity and the world—that will not be mandated by an economical logic.

In a treatise entirely devoted to the gift, or, more precisely, to the "kind deed" (*De Beneficiis*), Seneca appeals to the resources of a financial vocabulary in order to extract the gift from the economical categories of debt, return, and reimbursement. In other words, he tries to think the pure gift, the gift without return, the one Derrida considers as impossible, as the impossible. It is this gift that Seneca attempts to expose as central to moral thought—an effort that is ignored by Derrida and also by Mauss. Would not this Stoic approach to the gift have an enlightening effect on deconstruction as well as on anthropology?

The Gift without Return

It is not insignificant that Seneca's treatise on the kind deed (*beneficiis*) begins not with considerations on the virtue of generosity but with ingratitude. This is not to stigmatize the lack of gratitude, of acknowledgement, or of thanks (that the same Latin word *gratia* can express), but to prevent a moral misinterpretation concerning the expectation of a return. The ingratitude of the donee (the beneficiary) is not an obstacle for a kind deed, but, on the contrary, reveals the essence of the gift as the absence of return. "There is no loss because loss supposes calculation. Doing a kind deed is not a double accountancy. Charity contents itself by spending—if the obliged renders something it is pure gain, otherwise there is no loss. I gave this in order to give [*Ego illud dedi, ut darem*]" (I, 2, 3).

The sole financial comparison could reveal how we must not understand the gift. Above all it is the interest loans, the usurer's practices that are questionable. "May kind deed be, not interest loan [*Demus beneficia, non feneremus*]" (I, 1, 9). We can easily understand why it is the usurer and not the trader who is the focus. To buy and to sell are in no way similar to a gift. The exchange is carried out in the instant, without memory and without balance. The usurer, on the other hand, seems to give something, to abandon it, to get rid of it, even though he remembers that he did let go of it and that he can retake it again. And he retakes it with interest, increased by calculable fruits. The usurer is a false donor, a simulated benefactor, who acts as if he is giving, even though he calculates and anticipates a return. He serves as a negative model to reveal the perversion of the gift as well as its truth. "It is a disgraceful usurer's practice to bring into account as an advance, a kind deed" (I, 2, 3).

The financial model is not, however, the only counter to the true gift that expects no return. Beside the trader and the usurer, there is also the noble man who seeks fame, honor, and prestige in return for his kind deeds. In this case, it is remarkable that Seneca, in order to designate the gift, does not say *beneficium*, but *munus*, which has a completely different connotation, implying an excessive liberality, pompous generosity, public and ostentatious splendor. It is munificence. The gift as munus is not gift as beneficium. Its goal is not to help others, but is the triumph of the donor. He expresses his pride, his arrogance (*superbia*), and the result is nothing else but crushing the other, not the relieving of his pains. This regime of giving takes on an aspect of a struggle between the defeated and the victorious; it is competitive. It is a battle to obtain an award.

Neither the merchant exchange nor the agonistic munificence can, therefore, be retained as modalities of the gift. We must think of a third modality in which no return determines the act of giving, and where the only motive for the gift is worry for the other.

If no return is expected, it is not only the qualified ingratitude that reveals that the gift is truly a gift. More positively, there are situations listed by Seneca where the one who is provided for and helped is incapable of giving back. Nothing puts more light on the essence of generosity, nothing gives a better demonstration that it cannot lean on interest (*utilitas*) and on a vile calculation (what he names as *sordida computatio,* IV, 11, 2) than the kind deed given to the poor, to the dying person, to the traveler, to the stranger, to the unknown person. In all, these cases show the goal of the kind deed as precisely what it should be: "Not the profit [*lucrum*] nor the pleasure [*voluptatem*] or the fame [*gloriam*] of the one who gives" (IV, 11, 1), but the advantage (utilitas) of the one who receives. Interestingly enough, we will see the impact of these kinds of examples in an emerging religious teaching more or less contemporary with Seneca. Seneca articulated as a philosophical rationality what will appear in Christianity as a parabolic teaching.

The impossibility of return reveals the truth of the gift in separating it from the return and, most of all, in showing it as an act carried out for others. This service toward others must be the only reason (*causa*) for the kind deed. And yet the gift does not expect a reward or a salary, but it must also be accomplished, if that is necessary, against the interest (utilitas) of the one who gives it. In the kind deed, "someone who renders a service to others [*ut alteri prodesset*] often forgets his interest [*utilitatis*], ready and eager to give to others [*alteri dedit*] to divest oneself of goods [*ablaturus sibi*]" (V, 11, 2).

These three degrees of giving articulated by Seneca deserve our attention. It is evident that these three degrees are hierarchical. This structure repeats, by a necessity that we should interrogate, a staggering height from which Plato, followed by Aristotle, had already structured ethics. This structure proceeds from wealth to fame to knowledge; from merchant to noble to sage; from a life dedicated to material pleasures to one established in famous battles of the warrior or politician to a life devoted to philosophy and disinterested knowledge that, finally, includes the contemplation of the divine.

Most likely, this division embodies a necessity that travels beyond the cultural arena that formalized it. It is striking that anthropological investigation, open to the variety of cultures, cannot withdraw itself from it. It is remarkable that Maurice Godelier, in his recent essay *The Enigma of the Gift* (see also chapter 1 of this volume), evaluates and enriches the discoveries of Mauss by distinguishing three types of objects that inscribe themselves in the gift or exchange mechanism: sacred objects, gift objects as such, and marketable objects.

For Seneca, this hierarchical tripartition becomes the perspective from which to think a general logic of the gift and exchange: the beneficium (gift as kind deed), the munus (gift as action of munificence), and the *feneratio* (interest loan and all forms of the sordida computatio). It is only as a superior level in the gradation of the regimes of giving that the gift without return can be thought. This mode of giving imitates the Gods. We have two extreme positions on the moral scale, "The one who brings kind deeds imitates the Gods; the one who claims a payment imitates the usurers [*qui dat beneficia deos imitatur, qui repetit, feneratores*]" (III, 15, 4).

This very condensed expression quickly glances as a straight arrow going from one extreme to the other, helping to think the gift in its purity. And yet "God gives without any hope of return; he has no need for our gifts, as we are not in a state of giving any" (IV, 9, 1). The divine gifts are no matters of exchange.

I would like to stress that the *De Beneficiis* of Seneca is an admirable anticipation of the conceptualization of Mauss and, at the same time, a remarkable complication of the problem, that can be compared with the most acute statements of Derrida's deconstruction. We can be surprised that Mauss, who does not hesitate to quote obscure Roman jurors, does not mention Seneca. The Stoic philosopher thinks of the gift, or the kind deed, as "a practice that constitutes the most powerful link of human society [*quae maxime humanam societam adligat*]" (I, 4, 2). It is based on "the reciprocal obligation to give, to receive and to return [*commercio dandi, accipiendi, reddendi*] (I, 3, 8). The three operations of the gift that constitute the framework of Mauss's analysis are, thus, perfectly designated by Seneca.

But Seneca does not insist on the empirical description of that fundamental practice. He wishes to attain the level of principles and moral prescriptions that will be the consequence of these principles.

Yet it seems that all of Seneca's effort is directed at separating, by the largest gap, the sharpest discrepancy, the three actions of *dare, accipere, reddere* (to give, to receive, to return) to show their autonomy of principle, which makes possible the morality of the triple act of giving. The problem, for him, is to prescribe to the donor a giving without the hope of a return; and, on the other hand, concerning the beneficiary, a receiving and a returning that should not be confused with the reward of the giving or with a calculation to receive much more. Between the duty of giving and the duty of returning, there is not the symmetry of the trade, but the heterogeneity of two orders of reality.

If the act of giving accomplishes its essence with the ingratitude of the beneficiary or with this physical incapacity to return (the poor, the dying, the traveler, the unknown), this ingratitude or incapacity cannot be prescribed to the beneficiary as a duty. Therefore a moral duty on the part of the beneficiary is needed, a duty of gratitude, but that must be asymmetrical, not a simple logic of exchange of equivalents.

It is here that we accede to a conception that will be the essential moment of the ethic, a turning point in time. This new conception clearly distinguishes itself from the modalities that, in the anthropology of the gift, are customary to describe and to analyze. Between what is described by Mauss and what we think of the gift, we find Seneca already waiting, even though we have not read him.

Semiotics and the Gift

It is when Seneca thinks of the kind deed from the beneficiary's point of view that he develops a distinction that implies nothing less than a semiotics with important philosophical ramifications.

It is probably around that semiotics, inherent in the gift, that, unknowingly, the sharpest lines of argument are at stake regarding the ethical signification of the giving—even the very possibility of giving. Derrida's troubling affirmation that the gift is impossible (or, better, is *the* impossible) can be illuminated here, as well as criticized.

Seneca, who usually does not appreciate the tendency (too Greek, in his opinion) of making subtle distinctions that ultimately lose sight of a practical and moral thread of argumentation, cannot avoid questioning the definition of the gift (as kind deed). And he is, therefore, led to distinguish two or even three different meanings, to pinpoint three dimensions that are implied in the act of giving (the beneficium inadequately translated into English by "charity" or "kind deed").

According to the meaning of the word, the beneficium (the kind deed) is at the same time the object that is given (money, a house, a garment, advice) and the action of giving. The two things have the same name, but they have a very different impact and signification. There is the visible thing that is "the matter of the kind deed [*materiam beneficii*]" (I, 5, 1), and there is the kind deed in itself, the charitable action that cannot be touched by the hand, because "it is in the soul that all is happening [*res anino geritur*]" (I, 5, 10).

Evidently this difference is crucial to Seneca, and to all the Stoics. To confuse the two aspects, the one of the soul and the one of the object, the one of the matter and the one of the action, is to lack a proper understanding of the logic and the ethic of the gift. "There is a huge difference between the matter of the kind deed and the kind deed in itself; therefore it is not the gold, nor the silver, nor any of the most magnificent things that constitute the kind deed, but the sole intention [*voluntas*] of the one who gives" (I, 5, 2).

These two realities should be firmly distinguished one from another; they belong to two separate orders. On the one hand, we have the visible and material object that passes from hand to hand, which can be lost, found, or given to another person—similar to a commodity, capable of transmission and of possession—on the other hand, there is an immaterial reality that Seneca names voluntas, *anima,* or *mens,* usually translated as "intention." Yet it is this intention that constitutes the essence of the kind deed (*beneficium ipsum*), because it is only the intention that is good when something is given and not the object itself, as a material thing. According to the doctrine of Stoicism, a material thing is neither good nor bad, contrary to what the ignorant believe. What is important "is not the given thing but the intention [*mente*], because the kind deed does not consist in what is done or given, but in what is in the soul [anima] of the one who gives or acts" (I, 6, 1).

This conception is not strange to us. It does not radically surprise us. But we should measure precisely how, through different channels that we do not recognize, the Stoic philosophy became familiar to us. This distinction is not only philosophical. Even for Seneca it has a religious implication. It calls for a religion that would no longer put the sacrifice in the act of taking life and pouring streams of blood on altars. "The essence of the kind deed is found in what is given, in what goes from hand to hand; in the same way, it is not in the great victims, though they be very fat, with shiny gold horns, which resides the honor given to the gods, but in the pious and honest will of the one who venerates them [*recta ac pia voluntas venerantium*]" (I, 6, 3).

Therefore, the distinction of the two orders is a crucial principle to think the beneficium (the kind deed) in itself, beyond its material visibility. The intention is a key concept in Seneca's argument, with the difficulty, however, that the English word "intention" (or the French *intention*) translates three different words of Seneca's Latin vocabulary: *volontas* (will, project, feeling), *mens* (soul, intelligence, reason, dispositions, good heart) and *animus* (soul, mind, reason, judgement, desire).

Yet this distinction that lies at the core of Stoicism—consistent with the difference between the body and the soul, between what depends on us or what does not depend on us—also implies a semiotics. Here, what is at stake concerns modernity and postmodernity.

If the visible object of the gift is not the intention itself (which is the essence of the gift), this object nevertheless is a sign of the gift. Thus, an amount of money or a service given to someone out of generosity "are signs of services [*meritorem signa*] but not the services themselves" (I, 5, 1), because a kind deed cannot be touched by the hand—it is entirely of the order of the intention. What falls upon our eyes is in reality only a trace (*vestigium*) or a mark (*nota*) of the essential kind deed, which only concerns the soul.

When looking into the distinctions that the Stoic philosopher proposes in order to define the different meanings of the word *beneficium* (kind deed) it seems that not two, but three levels of reality have been situated. There is the object, there is the sign, and there is the meaning. At first a kind deed is shown to everyone's eyes as a material and visible object (an amount of money, a home, a garment). But this object is also a sign. It is the sign, visible itself, of an intention, a good will, and therefore sequesters an invisible meaning concerning the soul. In exploring the logic of the giving (which also will determine that of gratitude), Seneca is led to a ternary division. Yet it is remarkable (and very rich in consequences) that this division scrupulously takes on again the distinction between the signifier, the signified, and the referent of which the Stoics very precisely were the instigators. Accordingly, in the act of signification, there are three things to distinguish: the *signans*, the *signatum,* and the thing. Two of them are corporeal realities (the visible sign and the designated object); the other is a noncorporeal reality that the Greek Stoics named *lekton* (the meaning, the notion, the concept), intelligible reality, but not visible and not corporeal.

Yet it is this ternary conception of the act of signification, taken up to analyze the act of kind deed, as well as the act of gratitude, that enables us to think the dare-accipere-reddere, without reducing it to the interested exchange mechanism of the market logic or of the usurer's logic. The material kind deed is a sign of the intention (which constitutes the kind deed in itself) that points to this division, allowing us to think of this relation as an exchange, but, to a certain extent (and only to a certain extent), to dissociate the duty of charity from all return.

THE INCOMPUTABLE

There is no measure to account for the given and the returned. This is the contribution Seneca wins for Stoicism. We cannot place on a scale the given thing and the returned thing. In its essence, a gift is given from the soul to the soul. *Sufficit animus animo* (II, 31, 4). Thus, more than the gratitude of the soul, an object as a material sign of gratitude and of usefulness can be given. But the true return does not reside here. The return occurs as a grateful disposition with good will and true grace. It is, therefore, a new gift that will be made and not a return, if later on a new thing is given. It is not an exchange proper, but a relationship.

It would be necessary to analyze in much more detail than I am able here to present all the subtle resources that Seneca gains from the ternary distinction between the gift as signifier, the gift as signified, and the gift as a thing. For example, it is this distinction that enables us to say that we can return without gratitude and have gratitude without the return. In any case, it is not doubtful that it is on that ternary fundamental distinction that Seneca leans in order to extract the "to give—to receive—to return" from a marketing and usury logic, but also from the judiciary logic. It is also in accordance with this fundamental distinction that he tries to break the mechanism of the agonistic gift, the one that wants to crush instead of healing, the agonistic gift described by Mauss.

If gratitude as the gift mostly occurs on the level of the good will (*bona voluntas*) and is generated from a well-disposed soul, then it is no longer possible to lose materially in an exchange of gifts. It is not as it is in battle, says Seneca. For Seneca, "the will alone [voluntas] as long as it aims toward the good, should receive our praise" (V, 2, 2). This formula is very close to Kant, for whom "nothing can possibly be conceived in the world, or even out of it, which can be called good without qualification, except a Good Will" (Kant 1987, 17).

Thus it is not the quantity of material good given, but the good will to return that counts the most from the moral point of view. This is a will, however, that implies an active intention that can actualize itself, more or less, in a visible gift. Therefore, the ethic of the gift elaborated by the Stoics has this remarkable characteristic of making inoperative the battle of prestige analyzed by Mauss in the potlatch. The soul of the just remains invincible; it is the same in the matter of the gift:

> The one who has received gifts in greater quantities, of greater importance and most frequently: he is not held by that. The gifts given are perhaps fewer than the received, if we calculate what we give and what we receive [*si se data and accepta computes*], but if we compare the one who gives and the one who receives—and in them, it is solely the intention [*animi*] that must count—neither one nor the other will be the winners (V, 3, 3).

What can be placed in relation, or what can be compared, is not things but persons. And in each person what is essential and establishes the "self"—that is to say the soul—is the voluntas.

In introducing the ternary conception of the gift, Seneca makes the relationship of to give—to receive—to return incomputable. This relationship can no longer be taught, either on the economical model of the market exchange (usury) or on the agonistic model of rivalry. With this incommensurability of the giving and the return, the comparison that nurtured the battle of prestige disappears. There also disappears the possibility of referring to a common measure that could lead us to conceive the gift according to a market model. This is an ethical turning point. In reference to the tripartition of the gift regime, Seneca's task is to place the wise and other men on the most elevated and hierarchical level of the regime of giving. The one who is closer to divine donation, even if human weakness takes this ideal as a guide, can never hope to achieve it.

If giving and returning is a relationship between people and a comparison between things, there is no calculable equivalence. Once again, by way of a general equivalent we have the true gift at the extreme hierarchical opposite of the reimbursement of a loan with interest. Seneca tries to articulate, one to another, two or even three heterogeneous plans that are in relation but with-

out parallelism or coincidence. In a complex relationship of un-
defined and various modalities, the visible signifier of a
necessarily invisible and incorporeal signified (voluntas, animus,
mens) and the material object (substance of a gift as thing or
service) are referred one to another but do not coincide. These
differences extract the gift from the logic of exchanges in break-
ing every operation of the giving—receiving—returning. In its essence, the gift does not take place in the economical circle of the
return.

And all these returns (the rendered) do not come back to the
same and are not valued at the same level. Not only are some
regimes different, but they are placed in a hierarchy: an exchange
so interested that it is not a gift (trade, usury) is placed lower than
a gift so disinterested that it is not an exchange (the pure kind
deed).

And yet the approach to the gift by deconstruction (in reference to Jacques Derrida's *La fausse monnaie*), or the worry of
thinking the gift in the era that is designated (true or false) as a
postmodern moment, appears in its rigorous necessity. That the
thinking of the gift becomes, at a certain moment, difficult; that
the gift may appear impossible, or *the* impossible, this is the hidden consequence of Seneca's analysis that we just proposed. What
makes a gift a gift and all the logic of the dare-accipere-rendere
could not have been thought in their Stoic form, if not for the
horizon of a certain semiotic that is precisely the one that deconstruction wanted to undermine.

If the difference between the signifier, the signified, and the
referent is uncertain, as initially deconstruction sought to
show—if the idea of the pure signified, which is not the signifier
or the thing, belongs to a metaphysic that we must suspect and
deconstruct—then the gift is impossible. The gift is impossible
because it is, in its essence, if not in its phenomenality, of the
order of the signified. And the gift is even the impossible if the
voluntas is the signified itself or the ethic—as Kant maintained,
in the wake of the Stoics—that nothing in the world can be said
to be good, except a good will. It is that voluntas that we will never
see in itself, as such, in its true presence, but always through signs:
these gifts, these kind deeds, these presents that bring, in addition
to healing, are signs of a good will.

Indeed the suspicion is not illegitimate. Beside and before all deconstruction, it was feared that a rigorous distinction between two orders, the one of the voluntas and the one of the visible gift, would harden itself in a metaphysical and sterile separation of the order of phenomenon and the unknown noumenon, as in Kant. Or that the distinction would gradually deteriorate in the weak casuistry of a good will that was no more than a will without tending to completion.

A Founding Moment

The ethical Stoic moment, however, cannot be evaded in an attempt to think the gift. In comparison and in contrast with the gift of society described by anthropologists (Mauss, Lévi-Strauss, Godelier), the gift according to Seneca constitutes a turning point in which modernity is entirely engaged in a problematic form. This is the moment that the *conscientia* becomes the great witness, as found again in Rousseau's ethic. It is at this moment that the kind deed, in its principle, appeals and comes from man as a man, and not as a man identified by his status (*status*)—the naked man, says Seneca, whether free, slave, emancipated, king, or exiled (III, 18, 2).

It is then, without contradiction and contrary to the ancient and archaic ideas that certain individuals should be bound to others in an intransitive relationship, that the son can become the benefactor of his father, or the slave the benefactor of his master. To deny this, says Seneca, is to ignore "the human rights *(juris humani)*" (III, 18, 2). As we see it, it is a founding moment that contains rich and substantial ramifications, a system in which we are unable to touch certain premises without weakening the others.

It seems also that Seneca, at the same time evoking the problem (the ternary semiotic structure at stake in the semiotic of the gift), reveals the way to a solution. For Seneca there is also an impossible. But it is not the impossible of the gift, as it is according to Derrida. It is the impossibility to make a gift to oneself. What is accounted for is not the portion that necessarily returns to the donor, though it be in the sublime form of giving in order to give, or of a good conscience. What matters is the other.

The other is the cause of the gift, the essential otherness of the gift, around which all the paradoxes are woven. It is this otherness that situates the kind deed in a logic where it also finds its place in the financial exchange, usury and munificence. But it is also this otherness that can make the gift something other than the mechanism of exchange or of the gift-countergift, a worry concerning the other without a return. As it goes, the nonreturn is first and foremost a certain relation to the otherness of the other, and not a relation to oneself: a kind deed is for the "advantage of the one who receives it, and not our advantage" (IV, 13, 3). If the other receives a gift, then the gift takes place.

This no-return of the gift is first and foremost in a certain relation to alterity. The gift is not possible without others, says Seneca: *beneficium sine altero non est* (V, 10, 1). The gift cannot be a gift to oneself. On the opposite end, we can also formulate remarkable consequences that can only be rapidly suggested: there is no other without the gift. To give and to open oneself to the existence of others is the same thing. What the gift gives is the other. What Seneca demonstrates is how the possibility of the gift refutes solipsism. All consequent thought on the gift is, at the same time, a reflection on the modalities of alterity. We should be attentive to Seneca's insistence on that specific point: "No one can give except to the other; no one can be indebted except to the other; no one can return except to the other; this cannot be made by only one [*intra unum*]: two are always required" (V, 9, 4).

Translated by Marila Gackowski

BIBLIOGRAPHY

Derrida, Jacques. 1992. *Given Time.* Trans. P. Kamuf. Chicago: University of Chicago Press.

Kant, Immanuel. 1987. *Fundamental Principles of the Metaphysics of Morals.* Buffalo: Prometheus Books.

Mauss, Marcel. 1990. *The Gift: The Form and Reason for Exchange in Archaic Societies.* Trans. W. D. Halls. New York: Norton.

Seneca. 1935. "De Beneficiis," in *Seneca: Moral Essays*, vol. 3. Trans. John Basore. Cambridge: Harvard University Press.

8

Giving

Adriaan Peperzak

GIVING HAS become amazing (*thaumaston*) again. For many centuries the giving of the Law, the grace of the Messiah, and the gifts of the Spirit have occupied the minds of all those to whom the biblical tradition gives much to contemplate. Together with generosity, gratuitous benevolence, goodness, love (*philia, agap, amor, caritas*), and superabundance, giving has formed an all-encompassing horizon for Jewish and Christian theologians, from the time of Philo and Origen to today. However, one cannot say that giving and the gift played a major role in ancient Greek or modern philosophy. The reasons for this relative silence may emerge from a renewed consideration, but they cannot be formulated immediately. Recently, giving has attracted the philosophical attention of authors who, neither Hebrew nor Christian, but secular, "Greek," and enlightened, are puzzled by the unselfish aspects that giving and gifts seem to characterize.

If it is true that philosophy begins with amazement (*thaumazein*), it is no less true that thaumazein has various modulations.[1] The Greeks wondered about the phenomena of their *physis* and *kosmos* in a different manner than the Christians, who admired the Creator's grace in the book of nature; modern thinkers expressed still another style of surprise in their systems, while postmodern thinkers perceive the universe through a mist of aporias, paradoxes, contradictions, and "impossibilities."

In this contribution to the phenomenology of giving, I will take as my point of departure a remark of Emmanuel Levinas regarding the praxis or the "work" (*l'oeuvre*) of a life lived in the service of others: "*The Work conceived radically is a movement of the Same*

---

[1] Plato, *Theaetetus* 155; Aristotle, *Metaphysica* A 2, 982b11–13; Martin Heidegger, *Was ist das—die Philosophie?* (Pfullingen: Neske, 1963).

toward the Other which never returns to the Same. The Work thought
through all the way requires a radical generosity of the movement
which in the Same goes toward the Other. It consequently requires an *ingratitude* of the Other. Gratitude would be the return
of the movement to its origin" (Levinas 1972, 41; Levinas 1996,
49).[2]

It is typical for Levinas to describe dedication to the other as
an exodus without return. Abraham contra Ulysses. To live for
another is to live for another time, a time that is not one's own,
as is symbolized in the termination of Moses's life before he could
enter the promised land (Levinas 1972, 40, 42; Levinas 1996, 48,
50). The self-sacrificial character of asymmetric generosity is also
illustrated in a series of expressions that insist on being good "despite oneself" (*malgré soi*) and "against one's own will" (Levinas
1974, 176; Levinas 1981, 138). By giving food or time to others,
one creates a lack for oneself. Giving the "work" of a life yields
death for the giver.

By stating that gratitude would constitute a return of the giving
gesture to the giver and that ingratitude is, therefore, a condition
for genuine giving, Levinas employs a rhetorical device that he
himself has characterized as "emphatic" or "hyperbolic" (Levinas 1982, 141–43; Levinas 1974, 8 n. 4). As we will see, the quoted
passage cannot be understood as a logical or phenomenological
argument (gratitude or ingratitude come too late to alter the gesture of giving, in any case); it must be understood as an exagger-
ated expression of the radical independence that separates an
authentic gift from the thanks it might yield. Even in a philosophical text, such rhetorical exaggerations can be appreciated if their
irony is obvious and if they are not overworked.

Some post-Levinasian philosophers have made a similar exaggeration the core of their reflections about the "impossibility" of
giving, arguing that donation is inevitably trapped in the economy of mutually useful exchanges. Not only is giving destroyed by
gratitude, it is already annulled by the self-satisfaction or antici-
pated self-satisfaction of the giver. The numerous repetitions of

---

[2] Robert Bernasconi has already focused on this text in "What Goes Around
Comes Around: Derrida and Levinas on the Economy of the Gift and the Gift
of Genealogy," in Alan D. Schrift, ed. *The Logic of the Gift: Towards an Ethics of
Generosity* (New York: Routledge, 1997), 257.

this exaggeration have robbed it of its rhetorical charm and impact, but they have hardly strengthened the idea (or the *idée fixe*) contained in it. If the argument is right, it seems that one must choose between complete cynicism and a fideistic leap to the impossible possibility of generosity, giving, love, friendship, and so on.

My own amazement about giving is determined by three phenomena:

(1) The experience of genuine generosity;
(2) the frequent occurrence of hypocritical giving;
(3) the normalcy of mixed forms of giving.

Each of these points needs some initial clarification. I hope that every human being has experienced some form of genuine generosity demonstrated in dedication or giving; if this is not the case, one can always appeal to paradigmatic figures of literature, beliefs, and myths. For a phenomenology of giving, it is not necessary to establish that its purest form is an empirical fact; it is sufficient and necessary that we can imagine and think its pure form as a realizable possibility, even if the human condition shows us only contaminated or mixed realizations. A comparison between more or less generous givers, for instance, presupposes an idea of authentic giving.

That gestures and expressions of giving can be used as masks and lies, and that such use is frequent or even the rule in most societies, confronts us with several problems. Not only can authenticity be perverted, but the appearance of authenticity can serve the contrary of what giving suggests: by acting as a giver, we can seduce, subdue, blackmail, poison, slander, disqualify, destroy, and kill. On the other hand, if hypocrites are fond of the appearance of generosity, their lie pays a public tribute to the virtue they betray. They "give" themselves as "givers" in order to take things away from others. Stealing likes to wear the mask of donation. It must acknowledge the significance of goodness in order to succeed in its own obscurity.

That pure generosity is rare is not a revelation, but if this fact is denied or forgotten, we are easily led to believe that one must choose between extreme positions. If all the mixtures of generous giving and calculated self-interest are despised as unworthy of consideration, either giving must be completely pure or else there is no giving (or "giving" is the name for a special kind of egoism). If pure giving is not possible, however, we ought not try at all to be generous, because everybody, including ourselves, knows that in fact we are only taking and grabbing and being kind to ourselves alone. Raising the standard to heroic heights can both create an alibi for ourselves and justify our contempt for all attempts at generosity.

Wonder about giving culminates in the realization that a human life, for example my own, for the most part is given—in a strong but enigmatic sense of the word. This, then, I would like to add as a fourth, or encompassing, phenomenon contributing to my amazement. My language, education, communication with others, my participation in several cultures, my role in economy and politics, the shape and style of my life, my orientations, thoughts, and enjoyments, the fact that I am born and am still alive . . . all this is given to me. But is "all this" not equivalent to "me"? Am I, have I been given to myself? Am I not a most surprising phenomenon for myself? It sounds like a paradox. In any case, it demands a careful analysis.

Someone Gives a Gift to Someone

The activity of giving belongs to a group of activities that presuppose a subject, a dative, and a direct object: a giver gives a gift to someone who, through this giving, is invited (asked, urged, demanded, forced) to receive the gift. Another example of such activities is speaking: someone, the speaker, says something to a listener.[3]

None of the elements indicated here can be absent from the structure of giving, though each of them admits to many variations, including those in which the giver or the recipient remains absent, unknown, undetermined, only imagined, or fantastic.

The addressee to which a gift is directed is constitutive for all

---

[3] I have tried to give a succinct analysis of the dative structure as concretized in speaking in "L'adresse de la lettre," in Marco Olivetti, ed., *Religione, Parola, Scrittura* (Padova: CEDAM, 1992), 145–56.

giving. It would be a different activity if there were no one other than the giver. But can I not give anything to myself? I can, but only if there is some kind of real difference between me, the giver, and myself as the receiver of my gift. A non-addressed giving is a misnomer; it may be a throwing away or a form of detachment or liberation, but not a donation. However, the addressee can be almost anything: the machine that needs oil, the garden that needs water, a plant, a dog, a school, a tradition, history, the world, all of which can be invited to receive a contribution to their being.

The giver too can be many things. Not only can the sun, trees, and animals give, but also anonymous forces and unknown sources. Nature, Fortune, Destiny, Moira, the gods, or God may be experienced or imagined as givers; even a nameless giving, granting, releasing can be thought.

Giving without a giver is not possible, but the giver might remain hidden, unknown, indeterminable forever. If giving is indeed recognizable as such (and not just as an enigmatic occurrence or play), its orientation toward a recipient is essential. As I have already said, such an orientation implies an invitation to the real, meant, or imagined addressee.

This invitation (which can take many forms, ranging from kind suggestions to forceful insistence) includes an intended response: Please accept the gift that I offer you! However, it does not imply the necessity of acceptance. Whether the other accepts the gift or not does not change the structure of the giving. On the contrary, it is constitutive of the donative action that it does not depend on its effective acceptance. If the gift is refused, this might persuade a giver to modify her plan—she may, for example, stop giving because the intended benefit to the other cannot be realized— but nobody can retroactively undo the giving by rejecting or returning the gift. This is phenomenologically obvious when we compare a gift that has been refused with a gift that never arrived. They are different phenomena, but the giving is the same in both cases. Furthermore, an unaccepted or unreceived gift is as much a gift as one that is accepted. The intention that the gift be accepted, that is, the imagined and intended acceptance, is constitutive of giving, not the factual acceptance.

Is this simply a question of intentions and interiority? No, because all intentions are also phenomenal, though discernment is required to detect their genuine or disingenuous quality. Besides, what is wrong with interiority?

If effective acceptance is not essential, gratitude is even less constitutive. Whether ingratitude follows—and many gifts induce irritation, embarrassment, ungrateful thoughts, and poisoned responses—the intention and structure and phenomenality of genuine giving is not altered. If the expectation of gratitude motivates the "giving," this is indeed a veiled barter. The order of prior and posterior in giving and thanking is then reversed: someone seeks recognition or favors by imitating the appearance of unselfish generosity. A sharp eye recognizes the false character of such an invitation and responds to it with indulgence, contempt, false thanksgiving, or other forms of payment.

However, just as acceptance is natural and normal, and as such a normally expected response to the invitation implied in all donation, so is the expression of gratitude. All phenomena appear as invitations and suggestions; in a sensitive perceiver, they elicit an appropriate response. While the phenomenon of unselfish giving suggests thanking as an appropriate response, this has nothing to do with self-interested calculations on the part of the giver. It is a question of appropriate or befitting behavior.

The gift must be something that the giver "has." It can be an object of which the giver is the owner, but it can also be a word, a letter, a speech, attention, dedication, company, and so on. In some sense, it must be the giver's property, but it need not necessarily be detachable. In giving you my attention, I cannot separate my attention from me; in singing for you, I share my performance, my skills, my time with you. "To give you time" is a strange expression—as strange as "to have" or "to take" or "to possess time"—for it is obvious that I am neither the owner nor the master of time. I can only decide how I should use an available period of time. I can share a certain amount of time with you. If I "give" you my work, consolation, pleasure, or company, I share my presence or certain properties, talents, and actions with you. Can one conclude from this that such forms of giving cannot be completely generous, since in them I realize my own possibilities at least as much as yours?

Only a transfer that completely transforms something that is mine into "yours" seems to fully deserve the name of giving. But are not such transfers—giving food or usable goods—the least interesting examples of donation? Must all "mineness" be destroyed by its transformation into your property? Does giving exclude all kinds of sharing? How, then, could I give my time, my knowledge, my life? Is the ongoing dedication of someone who "gives her life for others" nothing else than a gradual suicide? Is one's interest in the life and well-being of others essentially opposed to the use of time and energy for one's own well-being and life? Or is genuine giving—and, for that matter, goodness, love, friendship, Fürsorge, devotion, and so on—compatible with, or even mutually inclusive of, authentic self-interest?

Here we encounter the classical problem of the relation between self-interest and interest for another, *philautia* and *philia, amor concupiscentiae* and *amor amicitiae*.[4] I would like to approach this problem by posing the question of whether the giver can coincide with the gift while maintaining the purest generosity in giving him- or herself to the other. But before we can answer this question, another must be posed: Is generosity possible at all? Suspicions have been sowed, and some postmodern authors, very much impressed by critical analyses of abnormal and normal behavior, social structures, economic mechanisms, linguistic and ideological patterns, have dogmatically affirmed that all human actions, even those that seem most generous, are selfish, egotistic, narcissistic.

One argument, at which I have already hinted, has been repeated over and over again for some time. It states that in giving, there is always some sort of payback: a reward, a price, a compensation, and that this annuls the unselfish altruism of the giving. Even if no one praises, rewards, gives thanks for or responds to the gift, the giver enjoys the satisfaction of her own generosity. This is the reward she grants herself, thus realizing her own interest in being decent and honorable.[5] The argument seems to presuppose that appreciation, as such, destroys the very essence or

---

[4] Cf. Aristotle, *Nicomachean Ethics,* VIII–IX; Aquinas, *Summa Theologica,* Ia IIae, question 26, article 4.

[5] It is not certain that Levinas would accept this argument as an elaboration of the following lines: "se savoir bon et, ainsi, perdre sa bonté" (Levinas 1974, 73).

structure of the appreciatable. Even simple awareness—if one perceives the generosity of giving—would annul its existence.

Do the defenders of this argument defend that true giving is necessarily ignored and unappreciated, never discovered, and forever unknown to anybody, including the very giver? Giving, then, must not be perceived, it should not appear in any way. Only if nobody knows about it, as a completely hidden non-phenomenon, can it be what we mean when we pronounce its name. Is giving then a noumenon, or not even that? In any case, one must not talk about it, not even under the pretext that it is a secret—because secrets are clearly given as puzzling phenomena. Giving would, then, disappear completely from the philosophical scene. Is this the reason that modern philosophy rarely talks about donation?

François Mauriac, in *La Pharisienne,* portrays someone utterly dedicated to charity for her own glory, and similar phenomena have been described by other novelists. I refer here to novels in order to prevent a behavioristic rejection of intentions and motivations. It is obvious that egoistic intentions can pervert every activity or disposition, including love, donation, praying, and consoling. However, the perverted character of perversions is as visible as the authenticity of unperverted loving, giving, praying, and so on. To perceive the difference, one needs discernment, which is a skill that must be learned. Even excellent actors can then be unmasked. In any case, the critique of giving as self-satisfaction acknowledges the decisive importance of intentions and interiority by building its case on the giver's intended satisfaction.

About the role of discernment there is much to say—too much for a thorough analysis within the limits of this chapter. A long tradition, ranging from the biblical prophets and pseudoprophets and from the Greek *sophoi* and Sophists to recent masters of spirituality, has analyzed the affective, practical, and theoretical conditions that must be fulfilled before one is capable of distinguishing the various spirits that inspire and motivate human behavior. To distinguish generosity from its most seductive imitations, or, in general, to distinguish the genuine from the fake, one's sensibility must be mature and refined; one must be experienced in detecting one's own and others half- and wholly hidden biases.

It is even more difficult to disentangle the various motifs that comprise the many mixtures of generosity and calculated self-interest that rule most societies. Social scientists and post-Hegelian philosophers have intensified the suspicions that have always accompanied the search for authenticity, but their own orientation was inspired by a desire to overcome the perversions of what they saw as genuine. Instead of relentlessly insisting on the impossibility of ideal purity, we could use their analyses to sharpen our perceptivity with regard to the mixed and messy character of most attempts. Mixtures do not preclude the possibility of greater purity. Instead of the static black or white of *possibilia* and *impossibilia* or the gray of their misty confusion, we need a theory of the multifaceted dynamics and degrees of catharsis. Could we please, for a while, tone down the rhetorics of hyperbole and superlatives to concentrate on the comparative of average lives?

Some arguments for the impossibility of giving display a lack of expertise in discernment, by skipping over the crucial difference between the occurrence of satisfaction that is the normal consequence of certain actions—which, therefore, may normally be expected—and a satisfaction that is intended as the "for the sake of which" of an action. That a generous person enjoys generous actions (including his own) is normal. But to consider myself generous because I know how to create the appearance of giving is perverse. The difference between both kinds of giving and (self-) satisfaction can be perceived. The narcissism of the imitation is confirmed by the voiced or voiceless boasting that permeates the actor's behavior, while the contentment of the genuine giver is neither self-concentrated nor without humbling perceptions of his own deficiencies. If the latter pays any attention to the good he did, he always knows that it is not good enough and, in any case, nothing extraordinary.

By imitating a gesture that is constitutively oriented to another's well-being in order to obtain my own satisfaction, I make the recipient a means for my own pleasure. Charity as a means for self-satisfaction destroys itself. But what is wrong with satisfaction?

If the enjoyable awareness of doing or having done something good annuls the goodness of the action, there are no good actions. Enjoyment naturally accompanies and follows the good. The suspicious argument that posits a contradiction between giv-

ing and the enjoyable response it yields seems to presuppose that
enjoyment pollutes the good, that indifference and suffering are
more unselfish than joy, that altruism is not enjoyable.

What sort of puritanism or morbidity lurks here? Can I not be
happy because you are happy? Am I an egoist because I approve
of my own actions? Should I, rather, be indifferent to my successes, or even unhappy with them? Must we reverse eudemonism
by deeming as indifferent or bad all actions that make us happy?
Does the good hate enjoyment? Cannot we be good if we like to
be good? If it is a condition for acting well that we do not feel
good about it, the best of all worlds is either awfully boring or
extremely painful and tragic. Does this explain the cheerless character of so many texts about generosity?

Perhaps the defenders of the argument are confused by the
idea that giving should involve pain and sacrifice. True, in giving
one's property, one "sacrifices" something that will be missed,
and if the other's suffering does not make me suffer, my generosity is superficial. However, suffering with the suffering does not
preclude rejoicing over all the good things that we share, including the other's and my own good deeds. Shared joy implies mutual and shared detachments; but the hardest part is the turn
from my narcissism to a position from which I am genuinely interested in, suffering for, and enjoying the well-being of the other.
This turn radically changes the giving gesture, by changing its
mode. Generosity is not proved by letting you have what belongs
to me if it is not supported by a cordial concern that makes your
existence central. To give you money or time can express many
moods and meanings. Benevolence—in attention, smiles,
warmth, words—generates different phenomena than a selfish at-
titude.

Are we capable of making a turn from egoism to concern for
others? Can a human individual be fundamentally "for the
other"? Is it possible to give oneself? Is it possible that the giver
and the gift become identical?

To Give Oneself

I can give what I have, but do I have myself? I have what I have
acquired, assimilated, integrated, or developed: a house, objects,

skills, work, texts, plans, and so on. But how much is received from others: parents, educators, guides, friends, texts, traditions, and history? As a participant in the overall economy, I give much of what I have received, but can I give all I am?

I can give time, attention, interest, and enjoyment to others, that is, I can share my time, my interest, and my enjoyment with others. But what about myself: can I give myself? I find myself and am affected by myself as totally dependent, inserted into the world, born and determined before I became aware of it. Awakening to myself, I become self-conscious, which is the beginning of a long, interminable journey of discovery and adjustment. What moves and motivates my search? Desire. But Desire teaches me adjustment, attunement, more or less appropriate responses to the phenomena through which the universe surprises me. Am I myself not the greatest surprise in all of this?

I am given to myself—without ever being able to convert this given into my property. I, my Self, elude me. Driven by Desire, this Self cannot identify with any of the desires that constitute the universal economy of giving and acceptance. My Self imposes itself on me, it is "given" as a gift that cannot be rejected or repressed. I myself, free and somewhat aware of who and how I am, must freely accept and achieve a mobilization that precedes all choice. I cannot escape this mobilization; I must accept it and choose it, but I can do this in various ways: gladly, sadly, with resignation or bitterness, tragically or enthusiastically.

Desire sends me on a search for the desirable—which, of course, cannot be found amid the goods and satisfactions of a universal economy. Nonetheless, Desire refers me to the multiplicity of desires in which I encounter the many possibilities of desirability—each of which suggests or invites or demands that I respond to its appearance in an appropriate way, by heeding and honoring, using, or admiring it as it deserves.

On the way, I discover my responsibility: other humans cannot be treated as elements, objects, or tools; their desirability demands respect, care, compassion, concern. I am responsible for the other; to-be-for-other(s) is constitutive of the Self that sends me forth. And this opens the gate for a new discovery: I am also responsible for myself.[6]

---

[6] I assume here that Levinas's phenomenology of responsibility can be

At this point, I should show how the asymmetric relationship to
the other—my being obligated by the other's face—also reveals
to me my own respectability and "height." I cannot here spell out
this deduction, but only indicate its principle. My similarity to you
and our radical equality is not revealed in the other's face, but in
our speaking. I cannot see my own face, but when you address me
in words, your speech provokes me to respond in a similar way.
In speaking to you I hear that I, like you, address, impress, and
order you by a demand similar to your demand regarding me.
Our equality is manifest in the similarity between your speaking
and my speaking.

The reciprocity of our conversation manifests a double asymmetry: just as your speech obligates me, so my speech obligates
you; your dignity awakens my responsibility, while my dignity
awakens yours. Two asymmetric but chiastic relations of high esteem intersect one another, thus forming a knot that binds us
together in responsibility. Our responsibility is unconditional,
but, since we are many, it is not unlimited, unless we can show
that my responsibility for you includes my responsibility for the
concrete realization of my own "height" and dignity. If so, I simultaneously serve your (true) interest and my own, because both
your true interest and my own concern that in us which imposes
itself on you and me as worthy of the highest esteem and care.

"Concern for the soul" (*meletētēs psychēs*) involves not only my
being-for-you; as *meletē heautou,* it also regards my own Self.[7] I myself am here for the Self in you and me, a Self that is unique in
you and separate from my Self, though it imposes itself in the
same superior way to you and me. I myself respect and serve my
own Self in respecting and serving yours. Concern for your Self
and concern for my own Self can coincide, because a difference
exists between the responsible self (you or me) and the Self that
provokes you and me to responsible concern for the dignity of
that very Self that precedes all choice and willed activity.

If the analysis sketched here is correct, we must conclude that

---

amended in the way that I argue for in *Beyond: The Philosophy of Emmanuel Levinas*
(Evanston: Northwestern University Press, 1997), 125–26, 176–77, and 226. A
double, chiastic asymmetry is not equivalent to symmetry or immediate equality,
however.

[7] Plato, *Alcibiades,* 127e–135e; *Apology,* 29e, 32d, 36c; *Phaedo,* 62d, 107c, 115b.

the asymmetry of my being-for-the-other is not abolished, but is duplicated by my own asymmetric respect and concern and interest for the Self in me. I discover in myself a Self that urges me to respond to all the surprising phenomena of the universe, including this very Self. How can I respond appropriately to my (always already) being moved, awakened, sent, urged to respondence? Do I respond appropriately by accepting, obeying, enjoying, thanking? But how could I obey or thank my own Self?

I can accept and enjoy it, and I always already am doing so, at least to some extent. But I am neither different enough to thank my Self, nor identical enough to possess it. Therefore, I cannot give away my very Self (including my inborn Desire and responsibility), but I can give all the time and work and desirable successes that are good for the splendor of the Self in others and in myself.

In order to better understand what has happened to me by being born into this universe, let us focus on the gift of time. "I will make time for you." "Now I have time to talk to you." "I spent much time on your request." Such expressions suggest that I give you time, although time is not in my possession. Since my conception time was given to me, and I hope that more time will be available, though rather soon my time will run out. This time, which is measured differently for you and for me, I cannot give away: in "giving" it to you, it still remains mine, given to me and through me, as my time, given to you.

Your time may or may not coincide with mine: during a conversation, our times seem to run concurrently, though even then, the shared time period relates differently to the rhythms of your life and my life. It is, however, also possible that I use my time for the good of someone who will live after my death. In any case, to give my time to others is to keep and live and "fill" this time as mine. However, in "giving" my time without losing it, it receives an orientation that it would not have if I lived for myself alone.

If the orientation toward you—your survival, education, refinement, culture, or happiness—is inscribed in the Desire that constitutes my Self, my "spending" this time for you is in line with the originary movement through which my Self makes me responsive to your emergence in the time of my life. Without expropriation, I let you, to whom I always already am directed, appropriate my time. A proper response to your demand identifies me with what my erotic responsibility has always already made me: a being-for-the-other.

Is it possible to give oneself, one's life, one's self, to others? I cannot give the erotic Self that makes me responsible, because it precedes all giving. If my life is equivalent to all the time that is given to me, can I then give my life? Yes, if all my dedication is oriented toward the cause or the people that occupy my interest—that is, if the entire motivation of all my "work" is in tune with the attunement through which the Self has marked me.

Therefore, to give my life or my time does not mean to bring a sacrifice by killing myself. I cannot "give" death, because death is nothing, but I can destroy another's life or my own. In giving my time, however, I do not destroy but convert the interest of my life to desirable causes that correspond well or badly to the Desire that motivates me.

But where is the pain, the "sacrifice," the suffering that are said to accompany all giving? They occur in the conversion from our mixed motivations to a less contaminated agreement with the Self, which, in attuning me, has made me responsive.

Responsive to what? Only to the human other whose face signifies to me an absolute demand? Above, I stated that my own Self deserves a similar respect for its absolute dignity. But I must extend my responsivity even further, namely to all the phenomena of the universe. Desire does not reject anything desirable; it is not fond of sacrifices, but seeks appropriate enjoyment and respect, justice, and well-attuned acceptance or refusal in proportion to the splendor or the horror of the phenomena that make me wonder. If all things, including my Self, are given to me, I am given to them as a respondent whose task it is to give each phenomenon its due according to the suggestions that only a well-developed discernment can distinguish.

Appropriate respondence, that is, correspondence, does not kill, but converts and purifies. A life spent honoring all things according to their due is a success and a joy, not only for others but also for oneself. Pain and suffering are inherent in the necessary purifications, but a specific kind of enjoyment cannot be withheld from affective and practical coincidence with the a-priori attunement of one's own Self. Dark but well-attuned nights are pregnant with delight, as the specialists of conversion—

mystics and saints—have repeated over and over again. *Gozo* (joy) and *gozar* (to enjoy), some of the most frequently used words in the texts of St. John of the Cross, characterize the mood of someone who has accepted all the suffering of history, while giving all his time and life to the Desirable that hides and shines in all phenomena as they give themselves to a well-attuned perceiver.[8] Amazement does not terminate in reflection; Desire transforms it into celebration.

BIBLIOGRAPHY

Levinas, Emmanuel. 1996. *Basic Philosophical Writings.* Bloomington: Indiana University Press.

———. 1982. *De Dieu qui vient à l'idée.* Paris: Vrin.

———. 1974. *Autrement qu'être ou au-delà de l'essence* [1981, *Otherwise Than Being or Beyond Essence,* trans. Alphonos Lingis]. The Hague: Martinus Nijhoff.

———. 1972. *Humanisme de l'autre homme.* Montpellier: Fata Morgana.

---

[8] Cf. *Subida del monte Carmelo* III, 16. *Noche oscura* II, 13.

CONTRIBUTORS

John D. Caputo holds the David R. Cook Chair of Philosophy at Villanova University. His most recent publications include *On Religion* (2001), *More Radical Hermeneutics: On Not Knowing Who We Are* (2000), *The Prayers and Tears of Jacques Derrida: Religion without Religion* (1997), *Deconstruction in a Nutshell: A Conversation with Jacques Derrida* (1997), and *Against Ethics: Contributions to a Poetics of Obligation with Constant Reference to Deconstruction* (1993). He has served as executive co-director of the Society for Phenomenology and Existential Philosophy and as president of the American Catholic Philosophical Association.

Maurice Godelier is the directeur d'études, École des hautes études en sciences sociales, Paris. He is the author of *The Enigma of the Gift* (1999), *The Mental and the Material: Thought, Economy, and Society* (1986), and *The Making of Great Men: Male Domination and Power among the New Guinea Baruya* (1986).

Jean-Joseph Goux is the Lawrence H. Favrot Professor of French Studies at Rice University and the author of *Frivolité de la valeur: Essai sur l'imaginaire du capitalisme* (2000), *The Coiners of Language* (1994), and *Oedipus, Philosopher* (1993).

George E. Marcus is chair of the Anthropology Department at Rice University. His publications include the Late Editions series of annuals, 1993–2000, *Lives in Trust: The Fortunes of Dynastic Families in Late Twentieth-Century America* (1992), *Anthropology As Cultural Critique: An Experimental Movement in the Human Sciences* (1986), and *Writing Culture* (1986).

Adriaan Peperzak is the Arthur J. Schmitt Professor of Philosophy at Loyola University of Chicago. His many works include *To the Other: An Introduction to the Philosophy of Emmanuel Levinas* (1993),

Platonic Transformations: With and after Hegel, Heidegger, and Levinas (1997), *Before Ethics* (1997), and *Beyond: The Philosophy of Emmanuel Levinas* (1997).

Mark C. Taylor is the Cluett Professor of Humanities and director of the Center for Technology in the Arts and Humanities at Williams College. His latest work includes *The Moment of Complexity: Emerging Network Culture* (2001), *About Religion: Economies of Faith in Virtual Cultures* (1999), *The Picture in Question: Mark Tansey and the Ends of Representation* (1999), *Hiding* (1996), and *Disfiguring: Art, Architecture, Religion* (1992).

Stephen A. Tyler, H. S. Autrey Professor of Anthropology at Rice University, is the author of *The Unspeakable* (1988) and *The Said and the Unsaid* (1978).

Genevieve Vaughan is director of the Center for the Study of Gift Economy in Austin, Texas, and the author of *Forgiving: A Feminist Criticism of Exchange* (1997).

Edith Wyschogrod is the J. Newton Rayzor Professor of Philosophy and Religion at Rice University. Her most recent works are *Emmanuel Levinas: The Problem of Ethical Metaphysics* (2000), *An Ethics of Remembering: History, Heterology, and the Nameless Others* (1998), and *Saints and Postmodernism: Revisioning Moral Philosophy*. Professor Wyschogrod is a past president of the American Academy of Religion.

Eric Boynton is a visiting assistant professor of philosophy and religion at Colgate University. His interests include the intersection of the philosophy of art and religion. He has published articles on the Continental philosophy of religion and aesthetics.

INDEX